PRAISE FOR *THE MAKING OF A CHRISTIAN BESTSELLER*

"I know of no other single source with as much professional wisdom and savvy as *The Making of a Christian Bestseller*. I will be giving this book to my classes, friends, seminars, and colleagues. There is no better way to understand the call and the cost, see inside the process and the craft, and get acquainted with the industry while rubbing shoulders with the decision makers."

—Timothy J. Beals
Writer, writing instructor, and president of Credo Communications

"Reading this book is like attending the writers' conference of your dreams from the comfort of your favorite chair. A must read for anyone who is serious about a writing career."

—Cyndy Salzmann
Multi-published author
and cofounder of
the Christian Authors Network

"Aspiring writers and seasoned authors alike will want to keep this engaging volume close at hand. Ann Byle's book abounds with invaluable inspiration and advice from authors, editors, agents, and publicists. Highly recommended!"

—David Sanford
President
Sanford Communications, Inc.

The Making of a
Christian Bestseller

An insider's Guide to Christian Publishing

by **Ann Byle**

The Making of a Christian Bestseller

An insider's Guide to Christian Publishing

Jerry Jenkins
Lauren Winner
Terri Blackstock
Karen Kingsbury
James Scott Bell
Randy Alcorn
Angela Hunt
Davis Bunn
Brandilyn Collins
Robin Jones Gunn
Melody Carlson
Sally Stuart
Charlene Ann Baumbich
Nancy Rue
Jack Cavanaugh
Robert & Lin Johnson
Barbara Nicolosi
Dennis Hensley
Wayne Thomas Batson
Jerry B. Jenkins
Debbie Macomber
Neta Jackson
Lisa Samson
Lisa Tawn Bergren
T. Davis Bunn
Bill Myers
Terri Kelly
Bob Hostetler
Jan Karon
Robin Lee Hatcher
Gene Edward Veith

FaithWalk
PUBLISHING
Grand Haven, Michigan

Printed in the United States of America
11 10 09 08 07 06   7 6 5 4 3 2 1

Library of Congress Cataloging-in-Publication Data

The making of a Christian bestseller / [compiled by] Ann E. Byle.—1st ed.
    p. cm.
  ISBN-13: 978-1-932902-57-0 (pbk. : alk. paper)
  ISBN-10: 1-932902-57-0 (pbk. : alk. paper)
  1. Christian literature—Authorship. 2. Christian literature—Publishing. I. Byle, Ann E.
  BR44.M35 2006
  808'.06623—dc22
                              2005030889

DEDICATION

To Jen Abbas, Shelly Beach, Angela Blycker,
Lorilee Craker, Tracy Groot, and Julie Johnson.
You do all things well as women, writers, and true kindred spirits.

Dedication

CONTENTS

Section Four
Know the Kids: Tapping into the Children's, Tween,
and Young Adult Markets

Section Five
Master the Specifics: Learning from Genre Experts

ACKNOWLEDGMENTS

Thanks, first of all, must go to the authors and publishing professionals who took time away from their work and family to talk with me for this book. It was a privilege and learning experience to speak with these gifted, dedicated people of God. Thanks also to the Writers Guild, those women who inspire and prod me; the Spirit Writers, whose gentle critiques and encouragement were vital; Candice and Randy Byle, who lent me their house for writing breaks; and to Sue Stenquist and Leslie Calabrese, who transcribed the interviews for this book and who offered me encouragement along the way.

To the people who have lent their backbone and personality to my writing career: Dr. Richard Cornelius at Bryan College, who taught me to go beyond what's required; Jerry Jenkins and the staff at Moody Press, who gave a fresh college graduate a chance; Ray Kwapil, who hired me as a copyeditor at *The Grand Rapids Press* and then let me stay; Wiley Stinnett, whose marketing genius is legendary; FaithWalk publisher Dirk Wierenga, who caught my vision and lent me his, along with his condo; and my parents, Dave and Shirley Egner. My father's love for words and teaching and my mother's drive for excellence are part of who I am. A special thanks goes to my sturdy husband, Ray, and my four children. They put up with a less than immaculate house, finding their own socks, and a mother who sits for hours at a computer. It is their hearts that are my own.

Finally, thanks to God, who created words and who is the Word.

INTRODUCTION

I found my inspiration for *The Making of a Christian Bestseller* between the flimsy covers of writers' magazines. Articles, columns, markets, letters to the editor—even the classifieds—draw me like a magnet. After years of reading major publications cover-to-cover each month, I finally asked the "What if … ?" question that conceived this book: "What if I talked to Christian authors, editors, agents, and other publishing folks about writing and the publication process, then compiled their responses into a book?"

I envisioned it as a digest that tapped into the experience and the knowledge of writing and publishing experts. It would put their expertise in one place, easily accessible to both beginning and more advanced writers.

Enter Dirk Wierenga and FaithWalk Publishing. I mentioned my still-infant idea to Dirk as I was writing an article about him and FaithWalk for the Religion section of *The Grand Rapids Press*. His response was positive; he offered several revisions on the original concept, then offered me a contract. That contract—my first!—was the beginning of the amazing process of writing a book. As a freelance writer for nearly a decade, I've written countless articles for the newspaper as well as for magazines, devotionals, and websites. Nothing, however, prepared me for the arduous, all-consuming task of writing something *much* longer than 1,500 words. I am accustomed to immediate gratification: Get the assignment, interview sources, write the story, see it published. Sometimes this takes only a week, sometimes a month or two. But a year or more?

Writing this book has been worth every minute of time and every ounce of energy. I've seen God open doors I thought impossible to budge. I've seen his plan come full circle.

Take, for instance, the chapter featuring Jerry Jenkins. It began right after I graduated from Bryan College in Dayton, Tennessee, with a degree in English. My first job was at Moody Press, now Moody Publishers, in the big city of Chicago. Among my bosses was Jerry Jenkins, long before he changed the Christian publishing world with the Left Behind series. I've interviewed him for the newspaper several times over the years when he visited Grand Rapids. I asked him to be part of *The Making of a Christian Bestseller*. He said yes, and I danced around my office.

Terri Blackstock came to Grand Rapids to visit Zondervan, her publisher. They contacted me, I interviewed her for *The Grand Rapids Press*, and then I asked her to be part of the book. She said yes and recommended I talk to Angela Elwell Hunt. Angie said yes, then recommended Brandilyn Collins, James Scott Bell, and Jack Cavanaugh. Jack suggested I contact his agent Steve Laube. Jim Bell gave me the phone number for Barbara Nicolosi. And on an on until I finally had to say "No more!" (Or I might still be interviewing.)

Grand Rapids is home to five publishing houses whose authors or editors are represented in this book: Baker/Revell, Eerdmans, Kregel, Zondervan, and Discovery House. This makes my hometown fertile ground for establishing relationships with editors and authors, many of whom helped me build chapters. When my work as a freelancer has me interviewing authors from these houses anyway, what else is there to do but ask them to be part of my book? It happened with Carol Rottman, Terri Blackstock, Damon Taylor, Regina Franklin, Lorilee Craker, Tracy Groot, Karen Kingsbury, and Carol Kent.

More than mere convenience or fortunate coincidence, however, crossing paths with these people allowed me to see how God's plan comes full circle every time. Granted, I may not see many of these circles come together immediately, but this project showed me that they do. I am grateful beyond words for God's leading in this book and in my life.

My dream is that *The Making of a Christian Bestseller* encourages beginning writers in their craft and in their quest to get published. I also hope that established writers come away challenged, rejuvenated, and ready to take the next step in their careers.

My prayer is that God uses you to help create full circles for others and that he completes them in you.

Ann Byle
October 2005

Jerry Jenkins
Terri Blackstock Lauren Winner
Karen Kingsbury
James Scott Bell Brandilyn Collins Angela Elwell Hunt Davis Bunn
Melody Carlson Sally Stuart Melody Carlson
Charlene Ann Baumbich
Jack Cavanaugh Nancy Rue
Barbara Nicolosi Justin Lookadoo
Dennis Hensley Dave Lambert & Lin Johnson

Pursue the Passion: Responding to God's Call to Write

Chapter 1

THE CALL TO WRITE

Carol Rottman

"Dear God,
Thank you for giving us stories that help us
discover meaning in our lives.
Give us boldness to tell them to people we care about.
Amen."

Carol Rottman never thought she'd be a writer. She has been a special education teacher, a social worker, a grant writer, a relief worker: a "cause-oriented" person, she likes to say.

What she discovered through the years of raising children, working for and serving others, was that she turned to the blank page in times of indecision, spiritual and personal upheaval, crisis, and joy. She invariably wrote her thoughts, prayers, and emotions.

"When I impulsively resigned from my position at a large public hospital, I finally began listening for God's call and claim on my life," she says. She soon started her own business, First Draft Consulting, in Cleveland, Ohio.

"I could not quit working, but by starting my own business I finally got some control over my work life. I began to respond to God's Spirit with my creative side."

After six years of writing for others via her business, she and her husband retired to rural Greenville, Michigan, to be near their children. She now writes every day, beginning each morning with prayer and meditation on a portion of Scripture, then writing her heart's response. That gets her started on her day's writing project.

"None of that is probably what I would use in my books, but it's the jump start I need to say, 'OK, my mind's ready.'"

Some of those writing projects appear in Rottman's first book, *Writers in the Spirit: Inspiration for Christian Writers* (FaithWalk Publishing). She's published some in journals, given other pieces to family and friends.

But how can a woman raised to believe service goes hand-in-hand with faith—a woman who believes work is ministry—come to a life of writing without guilt? Because Rottman began to recognize that God called her to write. The signs were subtle but unmistakable.

First, despite successful and interesting careers, Rottman was ready to leave it all behind. She'd overcome personal and professional obstacles to achieve success, yet felt no desire to stay. Her real desire was to write.

Second, writing was familiar. She'd been recording her "wild and wandering thoughts" for years. In the writing they finally made sense.

Third, Rottman received affirmation from friends, family, and the Christian community when she showed her work. Some of her essays were published in magazines and journals, and she began teaching a class at Calvin College's Calvin Academy for Lifelong Learning called "Telling Your Stories: Creating Memoir."

Finally, Rottman began to sense that God had given her both a voice and a message. That message is partly revealed in *Writers in the Spirit*.

"I approached it not as an expert but as a fellow struggler," she says. "The meditations and essays in the book are based on my own experience. I see my role, or spiritual gift, as an encourager of other writers, perhaps as a coach. There are a lot of people like myself who are reading everything they can get their hands on in order to be more faithful in the work that they're doing."

But writing as ministry? Writing as service?

"I have always maintained that the best service comes from something you're passionate about. It's better to channel what you know and can do into something very useful to other people," she says.

"Writing is not something that's unpleasant or dragged from me, but I do have an obligation to use that gift. I'm doing this out of faithfulness, though I don't know exactly where it will go and how it's going to help other people."

Rottman has struggled with what it means to be a Christian writer and the idea of writing "christianly." Should her work be different from that of a secular writer?

"I wanted to call myself a Christian writer, but I thought to myself, 'How is this different from anything a secular person would write?'"

It was friends who set her on the path to understanding.

"They said that my voice as a writer carries care and compassion, that it's like an act of kindness. It doesn't have to be identified as coming from a Christian heart.

"I'm very keen on the idea that, if your life has a purpose, everything you do is going to make a little more sense."

Rottman recognizes that writers face a number of obstacles she has faced herself. They range from fear to time, pride to form.

On time: "I meet all kinds of would-be writers who insist they don't have enough time, that their lives are too complicated. It's a conscious choice to protect the blocks of time that you have. I have many distractions—the telephone, my husband, having to cook, grandchildren—but I say, 'Nothing is going to take me away from here during this time.' If I'm fortunate, my writing session extends beyond that time. If not, it has to stop. But the idea is to start and keep the ideas flowing."

On personal essay: "In personal essay, the writer considers a phenomenon of any kind—whether it's a story, a fight, an interchange among people—and tries to make something of it. Why does that event make a difference to you? You're searching for a higher truth about what that story means to you. So it's not the story per se, but what the story did to you as a person."

On pride: "Is my writing good enough? I say it's good enough for today. You can't compare your writing to other people's, and you can't compare it to the unknown of what God expects from you. Humbly offer it, and it's good enough. God doesn't judge our size, shape, or beauty as making us good or bad. If writing is part of you, that's what God will love."

On fear: "Just do it. Get on with writing and let it pile up to the point where you say, 'If I wasn't a writer I couldn't have produced all this.' Then pick your encouragers carefully. My family believes writing to be a part of me and that takes away a lot of the fear. Have a few people who believe in you."

On non-assignment writing: "The writing itself is so uplifting. It proves that I can take these rattling thoughts that are always bounding around in my head and I can actually make sense of them. It's a wonderfully freeing thing. Instead of living in a frantic world, I live in a world that some days makes a little sense."

On creativity: "I believe that everyone is creative in some way, and that writing is just one form of creativity. God meant us to be creative, and he created us with a sense of making beauty and meaning from the raw material he gives us. Writing doesn't have to be good to be creative. It's still part of you that comes out and has its own goodness whether other people see it as good or not."

What if God calls us to write and we don't do it?

"I think our souls dry up just a bit," says Rottman.

Writing Challenges from *Writers in the Spirit*

1. Write about a person who has mentored you.

2. Look into your memory and find a person, place, or event to write about.

3. Write an essay, poem, or short story using 100 or fewer of your choicest words.

4. Take us into your writing place. Give the reader a tour of your mind or your pen at work, and the conditions necessary to make both work.

5. Write about a time when you faced a life crisis; show us how you searched for new meaning. Read your work to another person and let that person's comments be the basis for revisions.

6. Think of a rare experience you have had that few people have ever experienced. Share the moment. Take everything in. Recreate the time, place, feelings, and wonder of it all through words.

7. Think of a time when either a planned or an unexpected change left you feeling disoriented or alone. Write your story of such an event.

8. Write about the hardest job you have ever done in your life. What perspective did it give to your life-work?

9. Make two lists: one of things you love and the other of things you hate or despise. Choose what brings out your most powerful response and write fervently about it today.

10. Write a story about yourself as a writer.

Carol Rottman is currently working on a series of nature essays and, with her son, writing a book about the boating accident that left him paralyzed.

For more information about *Writers in the Spirit*, visit the publisher's website at www.faithwalkpub.com.

Chapter 2

Linda Andersen

NURTURING THE WRITING SPIRIT

Linda Andersen

"I think there is a creative well in writers that God put there. I don't know sometimes what I'm going to write until I begin and then find that the words in that well start coming out."

Creativity begins in the quiet.
Spirit solitude.
Interlude.

Linda Andersen lives by the clock of silence. It's what she calls nurturing the writing spirit.

Every writer needs times of solitude and silence, she says, time to refill the well of creativity, to rest and relax and refuel. It boils down to living an abundant life as a writer instead of merely a busy life.

"The writing heart needs solitude. If an idea is going to gestate and take root and come to fruition, it's going to happen more easily and creatively to a person who does not write back-to-back-to-back. The writer needs certain times of quietness and refreshment to refine and hone the writing spirit," she says.

Call them artist's breaks, space to breathe, time away. But get at least one a week, Andersen says, a ritual she practices herself for at least a couple of hours once a week. She walks along Lake Michigan, wanders the aisles of art stores, rests on her porch swing. One day a month she takes a day away at a nearby retreat house for solitude and spiritual renewal.

"I think the artist's spirit definitely needs refreshing, perhaps more often than most other occupations," she says.

Andersen has half-a-dozen books to her credit, including *Love Adds the Chocolate, Irresistible Lifestyles, The Too-Busy Book* (her most recent) and *Interludes*. *Interludes* offers about forty ways to insert cost-free, peaceful interludes into a busy life and make it more pleasurable, more abundant.

"My present passion for nurturing one's spirit by silence and solitude began with a search for simplicity as described in the Bible. Jesus spoke about 'the abundant life.' I didn't feel I had it, and I asked him what he meant. He answered over a period of years as I began taking short times away from regular work just to be with him and talk things over. I wanted the life Jesus promised in John 10:10: 'I am come that they may have life, and have it to the full.'

"Breaks allow a writer to be fruitfully unproductive, which I think is necessary to a writer. I began to accept the fact that my writing life would not look like the generally accepted American model of productivity. If it did, my writing would become dried out, cookie-cutter writing. I needed to let my heart wander, daydream, become receptive," she says.

"I think a true writer receives his or her ideas from the inner sanctum of heaven itself, from the Creator himself. And I have become convinced that regular times of solitude become the birthing room and comfortable cradle of all words later written."

Can't do it, you say. Family, deadlines, multiple projects at the same time. Back-to-back articles, chapters to write, loads of laundry, classes to teach.

Andersen sighs. She's been there before.

The mother of three and grandmother of five began her writing journey at about age twenty-five when she took an adult community education class with one child in school, two at home. She found that the writing assignments "touched something very deeply inside me that hadn't been touched before."

She began writing in earnest after that class, producing first one article, then another. She grew her writing slowly but steadily by writing articles for a local newspaper and a Christian women's magazine. She wrote a magazine column, and she began a freelance writing business. Added to that was speaking at women's events. But after twenty years of writing and at the height of her "busyness" came a bout with cancer.

The cancer forced her to slow down, to simplify her life. She didn't stop writing, however, and eventually produced the manuscript for *Interludes*.

"The simplicity I sought had been given to me wrapped in the unexpected package of cancer," she says.

She sent the *Interludes* manuscript out twenty-five times; it was rejected twenty-five times.

"That was all I could take. It was no longer fun, was in fact agony. With that last rejection I said, 'I'm going to quit this.' Trying to get published had taken all the joy out of it. I got in the car and drove to a beautiful country hilltop and I quit. The Lord and I had quite a conversation. It was very climactic for me. I came home and started taking my office apart; I put everything related to writing away."

Andersen calls that year away from writing her desert time. She began creating handmade greeting cards using pressed flowers, which she marketed at specialty stores.

"I started working with my hands for as many hours a day as I had been writing, and I loved it. It was so good for me," says Andersen

"I had a year of resting my mind and my heart. My strength began to return. My creative well was filled back up without me realizing it," she says.

Every writer has desert times, Andersen believes. Those times, however, are not to be feared.

"Writers should let those times happen and embrace them," Andersen says. "Embracing a desert time is more healthy and helpful and effective than resisting and forcing yourself to write stilted, cobwebby phrases and wooden words."

Interludes, quiet times, artist breaks aren't always easy in our world of deadlines, productivity, and rushing from activity to activity.

"I think it takes a very, very deliberate choice to receive and to make room for the creative spirit to grow in today's America," says Andersen. "There are times when I don't know what I'm going to write until I begin writing; then the words in that creative well start rising up."

Writing is a gift to be enjoyed, believes Andersen.

"The pleasure is in the pursuit, not in the attainment. I think a writer ought to write for herself, write what she believes, what she wants to write. If it gets to an editor and gets changed and is published that's OK. But if you don't get published I think writing is still viable; it's your gift."

Andersen believes that gift needs to be nurtured through deliberate quiet time and breaks from the craft.

"Look for those ways that work for you, that turn your mind loose from productivity, then make a choice to do them," says Andersen.

"Writing interludes give you room to hear the voice of God. His spirit has space, at last, to write from your innermost being and with joy."

Andersen's Favorite Ways to Nurture Her Writing Spirit:

1. Darken a room except for one candle, then play reflective music. Five minutes is good, but fifteen is even better.

2. Step outside and look at the stars for two minutes before going to bed. "There's something very helpful for the Christian writer because it puts us in perspective. It reminds us how small we are in comparison to the universe and yet how important we are in the eyes of God; it shrinks us down to size if we get a big head."

3. Visit a coffee shop, a quiet bookstore, an art store. Make sure you are alone.

4. Take a long, relaxing, candle-lit bath.

5. Sit cross-legged on a porch swing, surrounded by pillows.

6. Exchange houses for a day with a friend; sit on his or her porch swing.

7. Take a walk outside.

8. Experience an extended retreat in a place that nurtures your spirit.

Other Ways to Nurture the Writing Spirit:

1. Experience nature whatever way you can. If you don't live near a lake or the ocean, walk in the woods, through a meadow, in a park.

2. Visit a local arboretum or botanic garden.

3. Spend a night or even a weekend at a bed-and-breakfast, quaint hotel, or a friend's cottage. If you have a vacation home, visit alone.

4. Sit outside and wait for the first stars to appear.

5. Attend a local cultural event such as a symphony concert, a play, a ballet, or a musical.

6. Participate in a hobby such as woodworking, scrapbooking, painting, rollerblading, or baking.

Resources:
The Artist's Way by Julia Cameron
A Place For God by Timothy Jones
Invitation to Solitude and Silence by Ruth Haley Barton
Sabbath by Wayne Muller

Chapter 3

THE CHRISTIAN AS ARTIST
Davis Bunn

"If you're going to develop both as a disciple of Christ and as an artist, a deepening relationship with the Savior must be reflected in story structure, character development, dialogue and however else you choose to bring out the Christian moral."

What is it that makes Christian artists unique? Do Christians make art differently or make different art? Do we make art only for our Christian brothers and sisters or for the world as well?

Author Davis Bunn says there are two elements that fuel the need for art, whether it's a fine screenplay, musical composition, sculpture, painting, or novel. The first is what the market requires. What do people want to see, hear, or read? What are the trends or cultural norms that are fueling the art we make?

The second element is the personal drive of an artist. What is his or her driving force? What and how does he create? This varies from artist to artist, author to author.

"Unfortunately, most of the commercial art done in the twentieth century, be it from Hollywood or music or literature, has been fueled by pain," says Bunn. "Pain, rage, distress, and abandonment are the heartfelt themes of the vast majority of artists."

Christians, however, have a different view. It's not that pain, rage, and distress don't happen; it's that we've found a way beyond them.

"There needs to be a third element to our art, and that is the core issue of faith and what it has done to us and through us. This must resound in some way in the work we do as Christian artists," claims Bunn.

How faith resounds in any artist's work comes both naturally and through knowledge. Faith is part of the deepest core of a true believer; thus it is a natural part of a body of work. What is learned is the depth of the moral or message an artist illustrates in his or her work.

"If you're going to develop both as a disciple of Christ and as an artist, a deepening relationship with the Savior must be reflected in story structure, character development, dialogue, and however else you choose to bring out the Christian moral," says Davis. "These issues are learned, not necessarily through book knowledge, but through our deepening walk of faith."

One question such understanding prompts is whether it is mandatory for Christians to include their worldview in their work. Is it possible to be a Christian and not make faith, even at its most elemental, part of a piece of art? A better question might be, Is it sin to ignore one's faith in one's art?

"I cannot answer that. There are Christian authors working within the mainstream who do not feel any compulsion to express a spiritual sense of hope or divine imprint on their work, and I cannot tell you if that is sin or not. That would be a judgment on them as individuals and their artistic endeavors," says Bunn.

The question is answered more fully on a personal level. What has God called you to do, and how has he called you to do it?

"As Christians we are called to be salt and light in the world; however we choose to operate as that salt and light, whether as mainstream authors or full-on evangelical writers of message-driven fiction, is a question we must ask ourselves before God," says Bunn. "It is required of us to follow God's commands, but does this mean we must write overtly Christian, evangelical-toned stories? To me the answer is no."

It seems natural, then, that our growing relationship with God reflects in our growing ability as writers. We change spiritually, which prompts change in our desire to improve and grow. Change, however, is never easy. Bunn recalls hearing a pastor say that change isn't required in people of faith. It's enough that we are saved, that we achieved the success of salvation and eternal life. Bunn has seen the same thing in writers who achieve a certain level of success. Neither they nor their publishers nor their audience want to move away from what has proven successful in the past.

"Success is a stimulus for inertia," says Bunn. "But the fact is that the flaws we have as individuals are true and real and need to be addressed just as the flaws we have as artists are true and real and need to be addressed. It's far easier for the vast majority of people to grow as little as possible."

How far a Christian writer can roam is also a matter of individual taste and calling. Some authors, despite being people of faith, use themes of hopelessness and bitterness. Some successful mainstream authors today don't hide their faith, yet include profane language, violence, and sex in their work.

Again, says Bunn, it's not an issue of one writer judging another. It's an issue of how an individual author plays out her faith in her work.

"I'm not saying that what another author does is right or wrong. I'm saying I would have difficulty with the sex thing, but some of my books have quite a lot of violence. It's not graphic or gratuitous, which is where I draw the line, but in every instance the violence was integral to the plot and the spiritual moral."

Writers need only read the Bible for a good dose of violence and sex. The stories, however, serve to show us any number of moral lessons. Each story of adultery, war, death, and even rape illustrates a clear moral point ranging from God's judgment to his forgiveness.

"So can you have violence or sex without its being graphic or salacious? If yes, then I would say it's something you can justify, particularly to draw a very clear moral," says Bunn.

Swearing might be a different story, according to Bunn. Is swearing required from the standpoint of creating good art? Bunn recalls watching *Good Will Hunting*, a movie filled with swearing but with a strong moral point. Bunn watched the original, then watched a version of the movie with all the swearing removed. Was it still as good a movie? Absolutely.

"Dialogue up until the 1960s never had swear words," says Bunn. "Yet if you read Hemingway, Dickens, or Faulkner, the evil characters they created speak cleanly yet are dark and live forever as timeless, powerful characters. I think that can be true today. It's certainly easier to write a bad character if he uses foul words, but bad language doesn't necessarily make him a stronger bad character.

"I've actually written swear words in the first draft, but as I developed the bad character I took the words out because they weren't necessary any more."

As writers we must find how and where God calls us to write. Whether novels written for evangelical Christians or mainstream readers, whether nonfiction for conservatives or history for academics, the key is discerning how God calls each of us.

Questions to Consider   1. How is your faith informing your writing right now?

2. How is your spiritual growth reflected in your writing?

3. How has your writing improved lately?

4. Has success made you quit growing, improving, changing? Why or why not?

5. What lines have you drawn regarding violence, sex, swearing, or similar things in your work?

6. Why do you include sex, violence, and lack of faith in your work? Is it gratuitous or salacious, or does it play an integral role in your plot?

For more information:

www.davisbunn.com

www.thomasnelson.com

Chapter 4

Regina Franklin

PURSUING THE PASSION
Regina Franklin

*"Know that your message must be valuable to one person
before it can be valuable to many. ... If we're not willing to
share in the sphere of influence God has given us,
why would he give us a bigger sphere of influence?"*

Regina Franklin's first book began when she started to heal. This gentle, Southern mother turned inner pain and healing into *Who Calls Me Beautiful?*, her first book published by Discovery House Publishers. It is subtitled *Finding Our True Image in the Mirror of God.*

Franklin had struggled for years with body image, feeling that if she didn't look right or wasn't thin enough, she wasn't spiritual or loved by God. Finally she came to a point when she was plain tired of the battle. She was tired of hating herself.

"I was on spring break from my teaching job and was reading *A Fresh Brewed Life* by Nicole Johnson. Her chapter on beauty left me hungry. I came home one day and just started writing," says Franklin.

This was in 2000; she did not have chapters laid out until fall 2002. The time between was filled with writing, working, and having her second child. During that time, as she struggled with motherhood and her dream of creating a book for women, she had an epiphany.

"I didn't know who would even want my book. But one day my husband, who doesn't say things lightly, said to me, 'If you write this book, it will get published.' I wrote that down on a piece of paper, folded it up, and tucked it inside my jewelry box."

She didn't know how chapters went together and hadn't written anything longer than a 10-page paper in college. But she kept that promise close as she learned how to write a book, then later as the rejection letters piled up.

"I really felt the Lord impressing upon me that I needed to write. I really believe the Lord gave me that book," she says.

Franklin's story of how her book came to be published is one told in varying forms by many writers. It's a story of her own perseverance and patience, as well as her learning curve in the world of publishing.

In November 2002 she attended a conference with her husband, a youth pastor. Publishers had booths at the conference. She picked one, walked up and asked, "What does someone do if he or she has a manuscript that they want to get published? Should I get a literary agent?" The answer was a resounding No! Not yet!, but she did walk away with the name and e-mail address of an acquisition editor at the publishing house.

She lost it.

She wasn't sure how to handle the quotations from other writers that she used in the book, so she began e-mailing those authors. One gave her a contact name at a publishing house.

The publisher quickly rejected her manuscript.

That's when she began researching publishing companies on the Internet and via a directory of publishers.

"First of all, I read their statements of faith. I wanted to make sure that whatever company God opened the door to held the same beliefs about the Word that I did," she says.

She studied writers' guidelines for information on whether publishers wanted a full manuscript or just a few chapters, whether they even accepted unsolicited manuscripts. She also studied her father's extensive library to learn what books a publisher put out. She had a friend edit her manuscript, combing it for grammatical errors.

"Then I just started sending it out," she says. "I sent out around twenty solicitations and got back probably eighteen rejections. Discovery House responded positively."

Despite a positive response from another house, Franklin felt God's leading in sticking with Discovery House. The manuscript went through months of consideration.

"I got a call one night from an editor there and I danced for joy all over my house. All he told me is that they wanted to send my manuscript on to the full committee," she says with a laugh.

As her book wandered through the committee process at Discovery House, Franklin continued to grow spiritually and professionally as she blended her roles as wife, mother, and teacher. She sent the full manuscript off in May 2003, then waited for word. The waiting, she says, wasn't a huge deal. There were days of excitement, there were days of drudgery.

"It wasn't all-consuming. Most people around me didn't even know I was writing a book. I didn't want to live under other people's expectations. If God did this, he did it. If he chose not to work in that avenue, then at least I had written my story."

Franklin got a call from DHP editor Carol Holquist in late summer 2003 offering her a contract.

"I have told Carol often that I could not ask for a better company to work with. She says that there are bigger companies out there, but I say, 'But I know where your heart is and that means something to me.'"

Franklin has been interviewed on radio programs around the country, has seen her book used in the lives of women of all ages. She is working on a similar book for teenage girls at the request of Discovery House, to be released in 2006.

Her experience provides learning tools for all writers:

On Waiting to Hear from a Publisher: Once her book was in the publisher's hands, she didn't pick it up at all. She didn't look for sections to revise, didn't find picky things to change. In fact, because so few people knew about it, she didn't have to answer questions or offer updates. She stayed busy doing other things.

For Writers Who Have Nothing So Far but Passion: "First, 'Trust in the Lord with all your heart and lean not on your own understanding; commit your way to him and he will direct your path.'

"Second, know that your message must be valuable to one person before it can be valuable to many. Who cares if thousands of people know my story but there are women right around me who don't? If we're not willing to share in the sphere of influence God has given us, why would he give us a bigger sphere of influence?"

On Timing: The timing, she says, was God's alone. While she wanted to find a publisher earlier, some of the key

events in the book took place during the long dry spells of searching for one.

"I think that the length of time it took me to write the book was
really beneficial because I had to live out what I was writing," she
says. "I learned that as a writer I have to watch, because the Lord is
going to show me things I can use."

On Spiritual Growth: "Writing is a work in progress just as we are
spiritually a work in progress," says Frank-
lin. "I need to make sure that my life is speaking forth what God is
doing. I so often look at things in my life in terms of product. I can
be so practical that I miss the moment of something. I'm missing
the process of communication."

Her goal in life, she says, was not to write a book. It's an opportunity God opened up. While she walks most easily in her role as a
teacher, she is beginning to walk as a writer as well.

"It's important to understand that my primary call in life is to be
a witness of the Gospel, whatever form that takes. It may take the
form of teaching or writing; I am not defined by the thing I do but
by the work that Christ does *in* me."

A Word from Carol Holquist,   Franklin immediately caught
Publisher for Discovery House: publisher Carol Holquist's eye.
First of all, Franklin's unsolic-
ited manuscript showed her to be a good writer. It also revealed
faithfulness to the Scriptures, a passion for her topic, and a real
desire to write.

"She wrote from experience but could keep that experience in
perspective. She struck a nerve with a lot of women who feel they
just don't measure up," says Holquist. "She was able to tap into
that basic need, that deficit we all feel, and tell her story in a larger
framework. That is especially rare in a new writer."

Holquist also sensed Franklin's character, which shined throughout the publishing process. Franklin's request that if a picture was
used on the book that it be of a real person, not an airbrushed
fantasy, was especially telling. Holquist says also that Franklin wants
her message, not her name, to be the important thing.

"Regina genuinely seeks God and her character shows. She's
been gracious and appreciative of the little things," says Holquist.
"We're small, so we can't do the huge promotions some authors ex-

pect. She does her best, we do ours, and God will bring the blessing."

Who Calls Me Beautiful?, released in 2004, is in its second printing.

BEST SELLER TIP Discovery House Publishers was founded in 1988 as an extension of RBC Ministries based in Grand Rapids, Michigan. RBC Ministries is best known for its devotional *Our Daily Bread.* Discovery House's publishing list includes devotional books, Bible study materials and reference books, books about the spiritual life, commentaries, personal growth books, and books that address issues believers face in contemporary society.

Discovery House manages world rights to Oswald Chambers' material, which includes the world's best-selling devotional *My Utmost for His Highest,* as well as the rights to Ray Stedman's work. Half of all Discovery House profits go to supporting publishing interests in developing countries, including authors, publishers, and translators.

"We love to have new voices, but we're very selective," says publisher Carol Holquist. "Our books must be solidly evangelical, must feed the soul with the Word of God. We want writers who point us back to the Scripture."

Discovery House publishes twelve titles a year, with more than 200 on the backlist. See www.rbc.org/dhp/ for more information and writer's guidelines.

"We're a backlist publisher. We look for things that hopefully will be in print ten years from now," says Holquist.

Chapter 5

LIVING REAL AT THE TOP

Jerry Jenkins

*"It's helpful to remind yourself that media attention
is not coming because you're anything special, but rather
because your book somehow became noteworthy.
You have to continue doing what you were doing and not start
thinking the world has finally discovered you."*

Jerry Jenkins, author of the best-selling Left Behind series, answers questions about his writing, his success, and the Christian Writers Guild.

Question: *The Left Behind series has brought you media attention, from the cover of* Newsweek *to prime-time television interviews. How do you handle the media attention?*

Jerry: Despite having written more than a hundred books even before the Left Behind series, like any other author who hadn't had a breakout hit, I waited by the phone for even one radio interview. Now that Tyndale has assigned a full-time publicist to Left Behind and we actually turn down as many interviews as we accept, I'm never going to forget the lean days and start complaining about "too much media work." I see this as a season I will miss when it's over. You won't hear me saying, "Oh, no, not another network interview request!"

That said, hard as it is to turn down requests, if we weren't selective we'd get little else done. It's helpful to remind yourself that media attention is not coming because you're anything special, but rather because your book somehow became noteworthy. You have to continue doing what you were doing and not start thinking the world has finally discovered you.

Question: *What advice would you give other writers when dealing with the media?*

Jerry: It sounds like a cliché to say, "Be yourself," but there's truth to it. It may take some time and practice to forget how many people might be watching or listening, but you must simply talk one-on-one to the interviewer, conversationally, earnestly, and with passion. Inevitably you will look back and wish you'd said something more or different, but you can use those experiences for the next go-round. Hopefully, you get more articulate each time. And it's okay to learn to speak in sound bites. The media uses so little, percentage-wise, of what they record. *60 Minutes*, for instance, followed Dr. LaHaye and me to meetings, signings, and appearances in four different states, shot four hours worth of all that, plus interviews, and used just seconds in the end.

An example of how an answer evolves: I have come to surprising the general media by saying, "We realize our message can be divisive and even offensive in an age of pluralism and tolerance," then go on to say that we don't share it to offend but to inform, that we believe it and are not being condescending or judgmental. It's just that we feel this compulsion to give people this view of what the Bible says. I have learned to add phrases I know they will pick up on and usually use: sound-bite friendly stuff like, "We're not stupid. We know how this sounds. We realize our message ... ."

Question: *In what ways can media attention help or hurt a book, series, or author?*

Jerry: The adage that the only bad publicity is no publicity is largely true. For instance, Dr. LaHaye grew upset with Tyndale House for publishing fiction that seems to diametrically oppose the view of Left Behind. He's an articulate polemic and spoke his mind, and the media loved it. I stayed out of that fray, but the series actually benefited. That controversy alone brought Left Behind before the public afresh, and we saw a spike in sales. Go figure.

I have learned that the media love to copy themselves. If one critic says the books are mean-spirited or anti-Semitic or, my favorite, "gleeful" about unbelievers "getting theirs," the rest seem to parrot that without, of course, reading the books. Then you find yourself on the defensive. It's hard to tell what a book or books is or are *not*. So I stay on message, tell what we're trying to say, and if the interviewer starts with one of the mimicked critiques, I become dismissive. "Oh, that old saw from people who clearly haven't read what we've written. No, here's what the books say ... ."

One time on television they had the standard detractor, a college religion professor, who criticized Left Behind for predicting when the Rapture would occur (we don't, of course), urging people to sell everything they own (we don't), and wait on a hill to be rescued from this cold, cruel world. "They win. Everybody else loses, and they're happy about that."

I broke in and said, "I'm sorry. I was under the mistaken impression that the professor had actually read our books."

I feel we've had more than a dozen titles and more than a million words to state our case, so critics are free to say what they want, even when they're wrong or haven't read the books. It bothers me only when our motives are questioned. People who don't know us will claim we've milked the series for money, or wrote it only for profit, etcetera. That hurts, but you can't defend yourself by telling how wonderful you think you are.

Question: *What is the line, for Christians especially, between good and bad media attention?*

Jerry: Well, we would not be interviewed by girlie magazines for fear of appearing to condone their content, but we have tried to get our message to many venues where we know going in they will be hostile. You never know who's reading, watching, or listening who might at least discover we're not raving lunatics. I enjoy trying to at least surprise the audience in that way.

Question: *Beginning writers may feel a tug-of-war between the need to promote, or advertise, themselves and their work and the fear of appearing full of pride. What advice can you give these writers?*

Jerry: Accept every opportunity to speak passionately about something you devoted your life to writing. Don't talk about yourself. Talk about the work and the message. True humility shows through and cannot be faked. If you're proud and egotistical, your media appearances will backfire.

Question: *How does the verse that says "Pride goes before destruction" come into play regarding Christian writers and promoting their work?*

Jerry: "Pride goes before destruction and a haughty spirit before a fall" is a warning to anyone who thinks he has arrived because the media have discovered his work. Be grateful for it and use the opportunity to widen the audience. About 175,000 books were published last year alone. Only a minuscule fraction will break from the pack and be noticed, and much of that will be due to the creativity and hustle of the author. No question there's a fine line between being on the stump for your book and appearing to self-promote. But even that is worth talking about. Learn to say things like, "I'm not here to promote myself, but this message is something I care deeply about, and here's why … ."

Question: *What gives you the most satisfaction as a writer: a successfully completed project; positive reader feedback; pleasing the publisher; making enormous sums of money; honest dialogue with readers; using your success to help others?*

Jerry: All of those. It's not hard to pick one, however. That would be the second one listed, but let me take them in order. It's always *very* satisfying to finish. I often say, "Few writers really enjoy the writing. They enjoy having written." That's not original with me, of course. But writing is hard work. It can be grueling. That's why we're all—or most of us are—procrastinators. There's nothing like being done.

Positive reader feedback is a great reward, especially in the case of a blatantly evangelical project like the Left Behind series. Between Dr. LaHaye and me, we have heard personally from more than 3,000 people who tell us they have received Christ through reading these books. What could be better than that? It makes sales figures and royalty checks pale.

Pleasing the publisher is great, too, but that may just be a personality thing with me. I have always been a good employee because I like to support authority (within limits, of course). Having been an editor and a publisher, I know what they like and look for. My goal is to present as clean a manuscript as I can. That can start a buzz and warm feelings in a publishing house. It doesn't guarantee good sales, but it's a start. And if a title does take off, nothing thrills a publisher more.

I'm not going to pretend the money isn't great. I'd complain, but who'd listen? I know any writer would trade places and accept the problems of a best-selling writer. But having been raised modestly and as a Christian, there's dissonance between my biblical world view and having what most would consider unlimited means. I'm glad this happened when I was in my forties rather than my twenties, because who knows how I might have reacted to such a sudden windfall? I feel tremendous responsibility and accountability for the stewardship of the resources. I believe I will have to answer for every penny some day. And regardless what you do or don't do with such means, others have ideas of what they would do in the same situation and are glad to say so.

There's also the issue of people feeling they have a right to know what you're doing with the money. I'm not sure why it's only Christians who are asked such things. While there's a temptation to assure critics that you are being generous, Scripture is clear that if you talk about your giving in this life, that's your reward and you forfeit any heavenly benefit. I don't know what the heavenly reward might be, but I'd sure hate to jeopardize it.

Helping others is great fun, especially anonymously. We involved our kids in that and it's been a thrill to see them take those lessons into their own homes and families.

Honest dialogue with readers can be fun and invigorating, but for the most part, if someone disagrees, they will continue to do so. My goal is to thank them for caring enough to dialogue and to occasionally change someone's mind—if not about the subject at least about the author.

Question: *How do you handle your success?*

Jerry: I think it's important to remember who you are and who you're not. Having resources makes life much easier, and we like to share that with people. The best part is being mobile, being able to see loved ones and worry about things other than money. On the other hand, I've tried to give back by starting a film company and buying the Christian Writers Guild. Both of these are money drains, and meeting payroll every month for eight full-time employees, mentors, and part-timers has me worrying about it afresh.

Question: *How has the success of Left Behind changed you: your view of yourself as a writer, your place/role in the evangelical writing world, your relationship with God?*

Jerry: I hope I haven't changed. I count on family and friends to watch for that and be honest. The irony is that while any one of the more than twelve Left Behind titles has sold more than probably all the rest of my books put together, I didn't write it any differently. I have always given each project all I had to give it, so clearly the results are due to things other than my effort or talents. The right collaborator, the right idea, the right timing, the right publisher, the anointing of God: All these seem to work together. I can't say, "Now I've finally hit on the secret." All I can do is try to make everything I write better than the last, keep learning, keep growing, never arriving, and leave the results to God.

The danger in feeling materially self-sufficient is that you could think you have no more need for prayer, Bible study, church, and the other spiritual disciplines that should be there regardless of your income.

Question: *What obligation do you feel, in light of any monetary success, to repay the Christian community for their faith in you and your work?*

Jerry: That does weigh on me. I would feel this even more heavily if I were asking for donations. It seems to me that people who do that have to be very, very careful about where they live, how they live, what they drive, what they wear, where they vacation, what they own, and so forth. Though I do not have a donation-based ministry, I still feel that tension and the dichotomy between my faith and upbringing and our means. Thus we feel, for instance, that the government should not get more of our income than the Lord gets. And that we should not live conspicuously. You won't see us owning a yacht or homes in Europe. I'm not saying we give it all away or don't enjoy some of the excess, but as I say, we feel we are stewards of resources God has provided and that it all belongs to him.

Question: *Do you believe you work too much?*

Jerry: I don't, but I listen to the counsel of my wife and my chief of staff, who both think I do. I tend to internalize stress, and they might notice it before I do. My biggest failing is neglecting to schedule down time between big writing projects. To me, anything other than writing (such as media appearances, speaking, and traveling) is down time, but the fact is, I need crash time—at least a couple of weeks between deadlines to do nothing but veg. The old Protestant work ethic soon kicks in, though, and I start feeling guilty doing nothing. I really must get over that, because recharging the batteries is good stewardship, too. I'm learning slowly.

Question: *In what ways are you the same as and different from who you were before Left Behind?*

Jerry: That's a question probably better asked of others in my orbit. I hope I'm no different in character. My late father once said, "Success won't make you a better person. It will merely show you who you are." Having means magnifies your strengths and weaknesses. If you're stingy when you're poor, you'll be royally stingy when you're rich. Same with anger, pride, slothfulness, kindness, patience, and the like.

Question: *In what ways was Left Behind a watershed for you? The evangelical publishing world? Evangelical Christianity in general?*

Jerry: I hate to appear to be dodging this one, but frankly I haven't had time to think about it much. I know people talk about it, and it's gratifying to hear that perhaps the success of Left Behind has opened doors for others, revealed a market to general publishers and filmmakers, and so forth, but I'm not sure there's value in my dwelling on it. I'm grateful to have had a part in putting prophecy on the front burner for a season. Anything that gets people talking about Jesus and getting back into their Bibles and churches is something I want to be involved with.

Question: *What role do you feel the Christian Writers Guild plays in the Christian writing world?*

Jerry: I feel there is a place for us the way there is for other similar ministries, but that each has a niche. There are club-type writers groups for hobbyists, and those are great. There are low-key (and I don't mean that pejoratively) groups more modestly priced but every bit as helpful at getting budding writers started. We are trying to carve out the slice of the writing and publishing pie for people who want to devote themselves to becoming professional freelancers, making a living with their writing ministry. In one sense, we're not for hobbyists or people who want to dabble in it. We partner our students with widely published mentors who walk them through a 50-lesson, 2-year course that is doable but also asks a lot of the student. It's affordable but not cheap, and we don't apologize for that because we work hard at offering full value. It's a thrill to see new writers selling and publishing every day.

Question: *What are your goals for the Christian Writers Guild?*

Jerry: I want to restock the pool of Christian writers and see the level of competence rise. I want publishers to look forward to submissions by CWG students and members.

Question: *What goals have you set for yourself regarding your writing?*

Jerry: I don't sing or dance or preach; this is all I do. I want to be selective about the projects I take on and give them everything I've got, continuing to strive for excellence and to learn and grow. I don't expect lightning to strike twice in my life, so I have to deal with the fact that even great sales will look disappointing when compared to those of Left Behind. I have to remind myself that I am not responsible for that side of it. My job is to produce the most readable copy I can, trusting God to help me make the most of what he's given me.

Question: *What advice would you give aspiring writers?*

Jerry: Read a lot, write a lot, develop a thick skin. Study writing. And make sure those evaluating your writing are not confusing their love for you with real, professional objectivity.

Beyond the Book:
Evaluating the
Building Blocks

Chapter 6

GUIDING WRITERS TO BETTER CRAFT

Sally Stuart

"Though it's more difficult to get published, the final product is something we can be proud of. We are doing some beautiful magazines, some great publications for children and teens that rival anything they can get in the secular market, and that's encouraging."

T*he Christian Writers' Market Guide* is the top reference tool for Christian writers eager to find a market for a book or magazine article. Sally Stuart has kept writers up to date on the latest publishers, their needs and trends for more than twenty years. It's safe to say that Stuart knows the business.

"To be honest, it's much more difficult to get published in any form than when I started," says Stuart. "Years ago there weren't that many writers, so publishers didn't have that much to chose from. These days there are many more Christian writers, so publishers can be selective."

That ability to be selective means writers have to work harder to get a byline or a book contract. Stuart offers advice for both beginning and established writers.

First, a writer needs to determine what kind of writing she's going to do. Determining a direction is crucial.

"With a beginner sometimes it's trial and error, but find out what kind of thing you like to do, what you do well, and what sells. But at some point decide whether you'll focus on how-to articles, write on marriage or family, Christian education or whatever," says Stuart.

Second, a writer must build a reputation. Establishing credibility in a particular subject area is important, especially if you want to write a book.

"Too often writers want to jump to a book first but don't understand why, when nobody has heard of them or connects them to that topic, a publisher doesn't want to buy the book," says Stuart. She suggests first writing articles for magazines to help establish that credibility.

Book publishers are looking for authors who have some sort of platform in order to help sell the book. There needs to be some recognition, some tie to the topic about which you write. No, you don't have to become a household word. Just establish your name and get some experience.

"A lot of writers aren't willing to work at this. Good writers probably fall by the wayside because they don't have the persistence to stick with it until they've established that recognition," says Stuart.

It's similar in magazine writing: Magazine publishers often suggest that writers gain entrance to their pages through columns or by writing opinion pieces. Writers, however, envision a lead feature article, byline prominently displayed.

"Writers have to work their way in by showing what they can do and doing it very well," Stuart says.

A third requirement is research, something Stuart stresses every time she speaks to writers. Research means finding and following the magazine's writers' guidelines and reading past issues to discover the kind of articles it publishes and what it's recently published. Then offer the magazine an article within the suggested word count and with the appropriate slant.

"Too often writers do a generic article, then try to sell it to someone. You must figure out what the publisher wants and then write to meet that particular need. I tell writers it's like making a dress, then selling it door to door. That's ridiculous. You need to find out who wants the dress first, then find out the right size, color, and style. Writers need to know what the publisher wants and offer that."

Fourth, Stuart stresses the importance of attending writers' conferences. The benefits are many:

1. Establishing contact with editors. Often these contacts are the only way to reach a publishing house that doesn't accept freelance or unsolicited submissions. The results may not be immediate, but ongoing contact can yield contracts years later.

Many conferences provide appointment times with editors, though sometimes it's sitting with an editor at a meal that brings results. Before getting to the conference, research editors and their publishing houses or magazines to see what you can offer that fits within the guidelines. Write a proposal or an article if possible, making sure to present it as simply and quickly as possible.

"Direct and straightforward presentation gives the editor a pretty good idea of what you have, so they can respond as to whether they're interested or not," says Stuart. "Your destiny is pretty much in your hands at a conference, so seek editors out, and look for opportunities to bring up the topic you're interested in."

2. Instruction. Writers' conferences offer concentrated instruction by experts. You'll learn a lot in a short time about how to write, how the publishing process works, and trends in the industry.

An interesting sideline to workshop-style instruction is advice offered by editors who see your work. They may suggest you focus a little differently on the subject, may point out how your work might improve to better meet current needs.

"Those short conversations with editors can help you get your project into perspective, offer a better sense of what you need to do to make it a publishable project," says Stuart. "A lot can happen in those few minutes with an editor as you begin to build a relationship with him or her."

3. Networking. Not only will you meet other writers struggling as you are, you can meet potential sources for future articles. That aerospace engineer who wants to write a novel may be the perfect source for your article on metal alloys used in spacecraft. Networking with editors and conference planners can yield articles, helpful advice, and perhaps an invitation to speak at a future event.

New Options Available While the road to byline or book contract may be daunting, Stuart offers encouragement. She sees the Christian publishing world beginning to understand that it can compete with the secular market. While this puts large publishing houses in the market for the next megaseller, it opens the door for smaller publishers looking for writers with something significant to say.

"I think a lot of times writers try the major publishing houses but can't get their foot in the door, so they get discouraged. But they can certainly look at smaller publishers," says Stuart. She recommends looking closely at denominational publishers now opening their lines to books for the wider Christian Booksellers Association (CBA) market.

Subsidy publishing has also emerged as a viable option. To self publish a book was the kiss of death just ten years ago.

"Because the market has tightened so much and because there are really good writers who can't get in at a regular publisher, the industry has recognized that subsidy publishing is a route to take. For that reason, authors are getting the respect they deserve for a good product they produce," says Stuart.

It's also a way to establish a reputation and build a platform to promote your book. Self publishers often enjoy greater income than writers who receive only royalties from a regular publisher.

Stuart also sees publishers pushing Christians to deeper levels. It's an open market for deeper books for men, for example. She also sees Christian fiction continuing to grow in popularity, and fantasy and science fiction are waiting to break through. More publishers are also targeting African-American and Hispanic readers.

"On the questionnaire I send out for the market guide, I've noticed that each year there seem to be more and more publishers open to science fiction and fantasy," she says.

Stuart isn't so optimistic about magazine publishing. Magazines have a hard time maintaining a subscription base, a trend she blames on people getting their news and entertainment from television or the Internet. Also, articles tend to be shorter and use more sidebars, which Stuart attributes to shorter attention spans and less time to read.

That loss of subscription base means lack of funds to pay freelancers. Many accept no freelance submissions, choosing to assign all pieces.

"In an effort to draw in readers, magazines are trying to go with the big names. Articles with recognizable names are more likely to sell magazines," she says.

Stuart offers several suggestions for the writer eager to write for magazines. It's a familiar refrain, but one Stuart can't stress enough: "Be right on the mark as far as what you're offering because, if you're not, they'll find somebody who is. It's a matter of following the rules and paying attention to what a magazine wants," says Stuart. "Get the guidelines, read sample copies, and become familiar with the phases of the magazine market to know exactly who they are and what they want."

She also cautions writers to avoid sending out a piece before it's ready. If editing isn't your strength, find someone who can help, because editors are becoming less tolerant of misspelled words and bad grammar. Brushing up on grammar and basic writing skills is a must, as is staying on top of technology. Editors want queries and articles sent via e-mail, as e-mail attachments, or on disc or DVD. Typewritten articles or those written longhand on legal pads? No way.

And a willingness to be edited? Absolutely crucial.

"If a writer isn't willing to be edited, an editor is certainly not going to bother trying to work with him. We all need editing, and sometimes it's difficult, but I have found that I learned the most when I had a good editor show me how I could improve," says Stuart.

Brightening Horizons   There are certainly bright spots when it comes to Christian publishing. One is the growing respect for Christian publishing as a whole and for Christian writers.

"Though it's more difficult to get published, the final product is something we can be proud of. We are doing some beautiful magazines, some great publications for children and teens that rival anything they can get in the secular market, and that's encouraging," says Stuart.

She also finds encouraging the number of Christian writers' conferences, magazines, online help, and online support groups for writers. It's becoming easy to network with other writers via Internet chat rooms and writers' groups, a plus for writers who live in more isolated areas of the country.

"The Internet has revolutionized the whole writing process overnight," says Stuart. "Research is much easier. You can find information on almost everything quickly and easily. We're all connected to other writers, to publishers who put their writers guidelines on a website, to information."

The downside, according to Stuart, is that it may be too easy for writers to depend on Internet sources that may not be reliable. She recalls recently reading an online newsletter article listing religion editors at secular newspapers. She discovered the list was taken from her 1995 market guide.

"You have to figure out what sources you can depend on and which ones you can't. It takes extra vigilance to do primary research, not just depend on those Internet sources without digging a little deeper," she says.

For more information on *The Christian Writers' Market Guide,* visit www.stuartmarket.com. *The Christian Writers' Market Guide* is available at bookstores nationwide, or by visiting the website.

Chapter 7

Dennis Hensley
DRIVING BACKWARDS ON THE ROAD TO FREELANCE SUCCESS
Dennis Hensley

"A lot of people think of smaller ideas, then see if they can blow it up into something, but that makes for a very shallow book. ... How you make money is write the articles and sell them, sell the articles again, sell the book, then sell excerpts of the book."

D r. Dennis "Doc" Hensley thinks backwards. Many writers create a magazine article, then dream of how to grow it into a book. Hensley has the book idea first, then dreams up ways to market the chapters as articles.

"A lot of people think of smaller ideas, then see if they can blow it up into something, but that makes for a very shallow book," says Hensley. "I got into the habit of choosing a topic for a book, then I'd back up and say, 'Here are the ways I'm going to dice it up and sell each one of these parts to a variety of magazines.' How you make money is write the articles and sell them, sell the articles again, sell the book, then sell excerpts of the book."

His first book began as twelve columns on time management in a business magazine. The company paid him for the twelve columns, then paid him for the book, which came out in 1980.

While doing the columns and book, he became intrigued by people he interviewed who were not only time management experts but who worked twelve to fifteen hours a day, were in perfect health, loved their jobs and had marvelous families. That interest became *Positive Workaholism*, a bestseller that appeared in 1982.

"I found that these people, from major league baseball players to Loretta Lynn, had one common denominator: None of them ever went to work. They would have done it for free because they loved it so much," Hensley recalls. "That made me realize that writing is what I needed to do. I absolutely love writing, and that's it. It'll never be a job; it'll always be fun."

Hensley has now written about 3,000 articles, 150 short stories, and nearly forty books. He's a popular and busy writers' conference speaker, and heads the writing department at Taylor University in Fort Wayne, Indiana.

Write First,   His road to freelance success was backwards, too.
Learn Later   Most folks learn first, then write. Hensley wrote
                       first, then learned. He had the dream and the drive
to be a writer but hadn't mastered the basics.

It was a literary agent who finally set him straight. As a college student Hensley followed him around campus until the exasperated agent agreed to look at a manuscript.

"He picked up a red pen and said, 'I can tell you why nobody has ever read your manuscripts.' He told me I couldn't ever type anything single spaced, my margins were wrong, my lead was too long, sentences too long, transitions between paragraphs weren't good," says Hensley. "He butchered four or five pages. It was the saddest day of my life and the happiest day of my life. Finally, I knew what I was doing wrong."

That agent also suggested Hensley get some life experience, so he enlisted in the Army and fought in Vietnam. He journaled during his Army tenure, did some writing, and read voraciously.

When he came home he married his sweetheart, Rose, completed his M.A., and embarked with vigor on his writing career with small success. Then a mysterious illness left him hospitalized.

"I had to be put into the University of Michigan Hospital and I hated every minute of it. Then I discovered the book *Martin Eden* by Jack London and my whole life changed again," he says. "It's the thinly disguised autobiographical novel based on how London became the first person in history to make a million dollars from freelance writing. It was like the guy crawled into my head. I was addicted to that book."

Hensley learned the power of description, of using the five senses to create scenes. London could turn a flat, white winter landscape into prose of power and beauty.

"Here's a man looking at a blank canvas and he gets all that out of it? I've got this noisy, cacophonous, colorful world and I'm writing flat and dead prose? I deserve to be rejected," Hensley remembers saying to himself.

He realized he needed to hang around with writers and editors—folks who knew how to write, who knew what worked and what didn't. So he signed up for the Ph.D. program at Ball State University, did some teaching at the university, and got a job as a journalist at the Muncie *Star*. He wrote features, did play and book reviews, wrote a music column, interviewed celebrities. And every time he turned in copy the editors butchered it.

"They didn't have time to be kind because we were on deadline. I'd go back later and ask them what I'd done wrong. But this is what I'd been crying for my whole life. All of my writing got better," he says.

Hensley went on to build a growing freelance career, parlaying his love of music into writing for music magazines, his myriad newspaper bylines into stories for a variety of publications. He also learned to take advantage of every opportunity. Writing profiles of musicians for the *Grit* newspaper meant selling those profiles to music magazines. Getting to know music personalities yielded entree into the world of Hollywood. Writing for the business magazine yielded his first books, which led to other books by publishers such as HarperCollins and Thomas Nelson.

"I was really big into multiple marketing," says Hensley. "I'd take the same article and sell it sometimes twenty to twenty-five times. My all-time record was an article on how to be an effective listener. I sold it forty-seven different places and put it in three books."

He eventually left the Muncie *Star* to take a job as public information officer at Manchester College in Indiana. For four years he wrote articles for the alumni magazine and other college publications, wrote freelance, and finished up his Ph.D. on Jack London. He then turned to freelancing full time with a Ph.D. and two books to his credit.

Writer to Teacher (Backwards Again) These days Hensley is passing on his skills to new writers, another move some would call backwards. Instead of teaching first and then becoming a full-time writer, he took on his teaching role after finding success in the writing world.

"People ask me why I would give up writing successful books to become a college teacher, but it wasn't a sacrifice. I've done what I wanted to do and I have nothing left to prove. I teach because it's fun and I really enjoy it," he says with a laugh.

Doc Hensley's Advice

For beginning writers:

1. Find people who know the business and learn from them, whether in school or job settings, writers' conferences or seminars.

2. Network with other writers, because often those writers can throw jobs your way, co-author with you, advise you, or introduce you to others in the business.

3. Do something. No matter how raw or rough, write it down. Have faith in yourself. Just try it.

He shares his writing expertise, his marketing savvy, and his contacts with Taylor's undergrads, as excited when they make a sale or get a check as he was when he first started out.

"I enjoy getting to know the students, seeing them succeed, celebrating with them, and getting them to bond with other writers," he says.

Hensley is a teacher at heart. His advice for Christian writers today is pointed and strong: "Christian writers need to understand that what we used to call the 'gap' is much tighter today. When I started writing, Christian publishing was about ten years behind secular publishing. Now if you look at a trend in secular publishing, there's probably something already in the works in Christian publishing," he says.

Also, Christian readers are sophisticated consumers who watch television, go to movies, read magazines, have college degrees, and demand quality material. That puts good, sophisticated writers in high demand.

"Christian writers today assume they need to change their testimony and their approach in order to succeed. That just isn't true," says Hensley. "My students will sometimes turn in things with graphic sex scenes or off-color language. I tell them we don't have to write that way. We don't have to come down to that level.

BEST SELLER TIP — Doc Hensley's Advice

For attending writers' conferences:

1. Bring plenty of business cards to hand out, and collect plenty of business cards. This facilitates contacts later on.

2. Find a friend with whom you can swap notes or tapes from different workshops. This doubles what you learn at half the work.

3. Multitask. Research the area where the conference takes place, then write a travel article. Interview speakers or attendees and sell the article to a writers' magazine.

4. Choose wisely. Search for a conference tailored to your specific genre, whether inspirational, mystery, romance or something else.

5. Gather every handout, freebie, sample magazine, or writers' guidelines available. This saves postage and time later.

6. Put your face in front of editors. When you contact them later you can mention their workshop and how you talked to them afterward.

"I want to tell Christian artists, 'Don't drop your ethics and think that it's art.' It's not. Raise the bar."

His forecast for the future? More books for men and more Christian allegory.

For information on Taylor University's writing program, visit www.fw.taylor.edu.

Chapter 8

THINKING BEYOND THE BOOK
Lyn Cryderman

"The more an author can help a publisher catch a vision for ancillary products or other formats for the content, the better the chance to secure a publishing agreement."

No longer is a book just a book. Publishers such as Zondervan, where Lyn Cryderman is vice-president and publisher, are now acquiring what they call *content.*

"We're paying closer attention to the consumer; we let the consumer tell us how they want their content," Cryderman says.

That content may be delivered in standard book form; it could be delivered in audio book format, a journal, or a study guide. The point is, publishers are looking at a book idea as more than a traditional book.

Authors are just beginning to think beyond the book. Most, perhaps 90 percent according to Cryderman, haven't really thought about ancillary products that could tie in to their work. Zondervan, however, at least considers the possibility as early as publishing board discussions. The company will also consider ancillary products if a book exceeds sales expectations and seems to be hitting a nerve with readers.

"The more an author can help a publisher catch a vision for ancillary products or other formats for the content, the better the chance to secure a publishing agreement," says Cryderman. "We want to be good stewards with our resources, and a book idea is a resource. To see possibilities beyond a single book is helpful and good stewardship of that idea."

There are caveats of course. Some authors can neither generate nor sustain interest in a wide range of products—first-time authors especially, though that's not always true. And there's the issue of buyer fatigue and resentment. Too much product is a huge mistake.

"There has to be a good, sound publishing reason for doing ancillary products," says Cryderman. "If it's just to generate revenue, you're going to create resentment from everybody."

Cryderman says, too, that an author can say no to certain products. If she feels uncomfortable with note cards, for example, most publishers will back off.

"In the end we want to maintain great relationships with our authors. Even if it makes great sense, if it doesn't fit the author's character or personality or wishes and we can't persuade them otherwise, we completely back away from it."

The original book proposal is a good place to start thinking beyond the book. Judicious suggestions for additional products may spark publisher interest. Specific regional or niche market product suggestions may also prompt interest.

"There are times when I'm pleasantly surprised at an author's creativity in helping us have a vision for something we might have missed," Cryderman says. He warns authors, however, not to get the cart before the horse.

 Think beyond the book:

Audio book
Computer software
Inspirational gift cards
Greeting cards
Calendar
Journal
Study guide and leader's
    guide for small group study
Individual study guide
Curriculum for higher
    education
Student version of the book
Children's version of the book
Gift book edition

"The book is the horse. If it's a great book there's a good chance there will be some opportunities for other products."

Zondervan includes language addressing ancillary products in its boilerplate contract, which leaves open the possibility for the company. Authors rarely receive an advance on products, but they do receive royalties. Compensation is provided if authors must do additional work on the products, such as reading their book for audio editions.

Authors can also request a return of certain rights, audio rights for example, should the company decline to do such a product but the author decides to do it himself.

"Unless we think we're going to do it later on down the road, we don't withhold those rights. Most publishers are pretty generous that way," Cryderman says.

This trend seems to be burgeoning. The driving force, at least for Cryderman and Zondervan, is great content. Great content prompts interest in additional products.

"This makes good economic sense and it expands the influence and territory of the author. Any time you take content and put it in another format you're reaching a new reader," he says. "Retailers like it too because it generates more traffic.

Chapter 9

RESEARCHING THE DETAILS THAT BUILD A BOOK
Tracy Groot

"Research is the big arms around the story."

Tracy Groot is no egghead. She doesn't have an advanced degree in biblical history or, for that matter, a college degree. She has three young sons and helps her husband run their popular Holland, Michigan, coffee bar. Yet she creates novels steeped in biblical history and details of life in Jesus's day, with cultural background reflecting the turbulent politics of the time.

"I have to think like a really smart scholar, which scares me, so I have to do a lot of research," she says.

Layers of Research   One layer of research is what Groot calls "context." For her first two novels she learned as much as possible about what it was like to live in Jesus's time. She researched Jewish customs and history and studied the physical land of Israel during a week-long visit.

"The benefit of visiting where you're writing about is that you get a sense of place," says Groot. "Even 2,000 years later some things don't change. I learned about the temperature, the climate, and topography of Israel. I also think there is a cultural feeling from age to age that doesn't change, particularly in Palestine."

Another layer of research is what she calls "content." For *Madman*, her third novel, much of the context research had been done for her earlier books. This time she needed to focus on content. She needed to research Greek philosophy because the book is set in part at a school in Hippos, located on the east side of Galilee, which at that time was controlled by Greece. She also had to research demonic possession because one of her characters is the one from whom Jesus cast out 2,000 demons.

"I had to back way up because I did not have a good understanding of Greek roots, of who Socrates and Plato and Aristotle were, and how Rome tied into all that," Groot says. "I also had to learn about Alexander the Great because my main character, Tallis, is a fan of Alexander."

Wide Variety of Resources   Groot uses a variety of tools to research the context and content of her novels. Her favorites include the following:

Books. Groot finds books everywhere, from Barnes & Noble to websites dedicated to scholarly research. She's ordered them via the Internet, had books sent from other countries, and picked them up from the clearance table at bookstores.

"What's fun is that egghead books are usually cheap at bookstores," she says with a laugh. *The Atkins & Atkins Handbook to Life in Ancient Rome* I got from the used book section at Barnes & Noble."

Her first step is to get hold of several books she knows she must have, then move on from there. "Start with one good book. That book will lead you to another book, to another and another. Your brain will leap on to different things you need to cover and research."

A basic Bible handbook is a good place to start, but topic-specific books are best. For example, her understanding of Greek thought and culture was deepened by the book *Alexander to Actium: Historical Evolution of the Hellenistic Age. Women in Monarchy in Macedonia* helped her gather background on Alexander's mother, who was from Macedonia.

Groot marks them up with highlighter, dog-ears pages, and takes notes on the information she needs. Some books yield much, others just a little. But it's the tiniest details that lend authenticity to Groot's tales.

She also uses the library to find books that may contain that piece of information she needs. Coffee table books provide stunning images as well. From the book *Israel from the Air* she was able to glean information on the winding route of the Jordan River. Another source is book clubs dedicated to your area of interest.

Websites. In this Internet era, websites offer researchers loads of information on countless topics. Groot uses a search engine to get a list of possible resources, then finds those that seem most interesting. These could be general websites on biblical history or more scholarly sites put together by universities or professional organizations. She has also ordered books from websites.

One caution, however, is that endless web searching can sap the time you need to spend writing. Groot also didn't research demon possession on the web because she knew any visit to such a site could bring endless and definitely unwanted spam e-mail.

Maps. Maps are key to recreating the topography of an area, to learning distances between towns or places, even to discovering different names of cities. *The Historical Atlas of the Classical World* is an invaluable resource for picturing the world as it was in ancient times, according to Groot. Maps are available from a variety of sources, including a Bible, Bible handbook, atlas, and websites.

DVDs and/or CDs. Groot got hold of a DVD featuring the land of Israel, the first in a series called *Pictorial Library of Bible Lands* (www.bibleplaces.com). It provided her with visual images of the areas in Israel she needed information on, especially valuable because she wasn't able to make another trip due to political unrest. DVDs are available on many topics through a variety of sources.

Scholarly journals and materials. Groot used the Internet to track down a number of scholarly articles appearing in peer-reviewed journals that were integral to her research (use a university library if you don't have access to these). One such piece was the excavation report of the city of Kursi, where Jesus expelled the demons. The report, put out by the Israel Antiquities Authority, detailed the ancient city's topography, worship practices, commercial practices, and even commented on the miracle of the demoniac.

Site visits. Groot's trip to Israel provided her with vast amounts of information on Palestine. She visited a village recreated as it would have been in Jesus's day, taking notes on how pottery was placed in the floor, on cooking utensils, window ledges, farming equipment, and even clothing styles. Many of these details made it into the books.

She also made a whirlwind trip to Toronto when the so-called James ossuary was on display at the Royal Ontario Museum. The bone box is inscribed with "James, son of Joseph, brother of Jesus," and is thought by many experts to be the repository of the bones of James, the subject of Groot's first book.

Movies. Groot watched *The Exorcist* as research for *Madman* (not before praying through every room of her house) and *Gladiator* to see visual images of Rome and its soldiers to augment her book learning.

"Books didn't give me things like firelight glinting off armor, or unshaven men with gray teeth—and when I saw them unshaven, I naturally thought they might smell a little, too. Visual research is incredibly valuable; one thing always leads to another; your imagination already leaping onto what the eyes suggest," she says.

Sometimes Hollywood gets it right, Groot says, while other times the movies are bad renditions at best, so watch each one with circumspection. Libraries are useful for finding a broad range of movies about specific time periods.

Personal interviews. Interviews can be especially useful for those writing modern novels. Take good notes and tape the interview if possible. Find interview sources through the Internet, chat rooms, friends, acquaintances, and even the phone book.

Other sources: Magazines, television interviews, DVD or hard copy encyclopedia, dictionaries, old manuscripts, museums, and hands-on work. Groot needed to find out how an ancient oil lamp might look as it burned, so she used one she had purchased in Israel, filled it with olive oil and a wick, and watched the light flicker in her dark kitchen.

Research Questions and Answers

How can I get through all these details? "Sometimes when you plow through the dry stuff you find nuggets. I consider myself an amateur archaeologist; shuffling through the debris I might find one significant thing. So go ahead and plow through the dry stuff; if anything it builds character. Anything you do is going to end up serving you somehow."

Is there more to research than just details? "You begin to develop your characters as you research. It's not as if your story is dying as it waits to be written. Your story is being written as you research. Your characters, too, begin as sketches in your brain but get colored in as you research."

How do you keep track of your notes? Groot maps out her general research plan and research goals for each day. She writes down every source she uses in a notebook dedicated to the novel she's working on. She can look back and know what she did each day: which source she studied, how many pages she read, what questions she has. Information she gleans is divided by subject and put into separate file folders.

"First I read a chapter and highlight as I go. Then I go back and write down everything I highlighted, focusing on what struck me in a particular chapter and recording that. When it comes time to start incorporating story line, I read the notes once again," she says.

How do you keep track of all the scenes in your novels? "I use color-coded scene cards. For every scene I write, I put a short synopsis on the card, plus research information. I usually do this after I've written about half the book so that I can get a bird's-eye view of the whole story."

She color codes the cards according to each character and puts them in order. This allows her to see who is the focus of each scene, and if one character is dominating the novel.

What if I hate research? Too bad. If you want to write a novel, especially historical fiction, research is involved.

"If you had told me I would be reading all this stuff I would have said forget it. But one thing leads to another. Once you're into it, you're either so fascinated or so caught up in the research that you end up doing your job. There's no way you're going to stop until it's finished."

How do you know when to stop researching and start writing? Groot admits to occasionally having done too much research. She found *Madman* too heavy with information on Alexander the Great, so she chopped much of it out. She found herself spending too much time on the Nicean Creed when it was unnecessary to the plot.

"I always tell myself that every stone must be turned," says Groot. "When to start writing is one of those things you really can't convey. You just know when you're done."

What if the research contradicts itself? Pick the best source and use it as your base. Often historical research is inconclusive, so don't get too tied in a knot.

Tracy Groot's Top Research Tips

1. Have a clear sense of place. Narrow down the place on which your novel is based, then research accordingly.

2. Develop a sense of culture. Back up 500 years from your chosen time period and place so that you can come in to your story having a sense of the cultural and political feeling of the time.

3. Have a sense of context. What materials were used to make serving bowls? What were they eating then? What were they wearing? Be especially careful that details are accurate.

4. Use a variety of sources. "You're handicapping yourself if you don't avail yourself of all the different sources available," says Groot.

5. Pay your dues. Know what you're getting into and be willing to do it.

"Not every reader is going to appreciate the research you did; in fact, the great majority of readers only care about the story. But there wouldn't be a story without research and the story is what matters. Research is the big arms around the story."

For more information on Tracy Groot, visit www.tracygroot.com. For information on Moody Publishers, visit www.moodypublishers.com.

BEST SELLER TIP

One Writer's Journey

Tracy Groot dreamed of being a writer until she became a Christian. At age sixteen she came to know Christ and gave up the dream she'd had since age eight.

"The whole Christian thing blew me away. I was having so much fun that all my writing went out the window. I was, literally, this hippie Jesus freak for a couple of years," Groot says, laughing. "Then I realized that the very thing he gifted me with is where he wanted me to go."

So Groot, by now in her mid-twenties, took up writing once more, forgoing college to work instead. She got married and started a family. She worked in the accounting department for a large corporation, then at a radio station writing commercials. She joined a writers' group—"big on dreams, short on reality"—wrote a few articles for magazines, and began messing around with stories for kids.

She had two young adult mystery novels published, but it was a request from her pastor to write a play that really got her started on her present career as a writer of biblical fiction. That request for a play on James, the brother of Jesus, grew into Groot's first adult novel, *The Brother's Keeper*, released in 2003 by Moody Publishers. Her second novel, *Stones of My Accusers*, was released in 2004. Her third novel, *Madman* was released in 2006. She's currently working on a science fiction novel.

Chapter 10

A Hard Look at Self Publishing

Carmen Leal

*"The rule of thumb is that if you can sell 1,000 copies in a year
and you're not going to borrow money to do so,
you are a decent candidate for self publishing."*

Carmen Leal began her writing career in a most unlikely fashion: She used a fleece. She felt God's tug on her heart to write a book about Huntington's disease, an inherited disease that was slowly incapacitating her husband of less than three years.

A book, however, was the last thing on her mind. "I laughed at God and screamed at him and cried at him and finally said 'Fine,'" Leal recalls.

First she tried to get Huntington's experts to write the book. Not one person would. Then came the fleece. Carmen told God that she would write one article and send it to one magazine. If that article was published, she'd write the Huntington's book.

So Leal, owner of a marketing firm and caregiver of a spouse with Huntington's, wrote a story about a dog and sent it to a Focus on the Family magazine for single parents. It was single-spaced and double-sided, contained no contact information and no self-addressed, stamped envelope.

"Eight days later I got a contract that said they'd pay me a hundred dollars. Words cannot describe how mad I was," she says with a laugh. "But a fleece is a fleece so I said, 'OK God, I'll write you a book.'"

Leal knew several things. First, she knew enough about marketing to understand that she was creating a product, not just writing a book. She also knew she would have to self publish her book. With only about 30,000 people in the country suffering from Huntington's and because it's a family disease so people could pass the book around, the market was too small for a traditional publisher to pick it up.

She joined an online support group for people dealing with Huntington's, putting out a call for stories. She was inundated. She gathered stories and data, then her son helped her create a website for the book. A professional editor volunteered to edit the manuscript, a cover designer offered her services, and, finally, a Huntington's caregiver volunteered to lend her the money for printing costs.

Essence printed 6,000 books in 1998. She has sold every copy of *Faces of Huntington's*. She's planning now to reprint the book.

She has also self published *Pinches of Salt, Prisms of Light* (Essence, 1999) and *Portraits of Huntington's: Choosing Joy Through Life Lessons* (Essence, 2001).

"The rule of thumb is that if you can sell 1,000 copies in a year and you're not going to borrow money to do so, you are a decent candidate for self publishing," Leal says.

She offers several good reasons to consider self publishing. First is what she calls the difference between a long-haul writer and a short-haul writer.

"I was a short-haul writer. All I cared about was getting this book into the marketplace because I was passionate about it. Self publishing is great for that," she says.

Self publishing is a good plan if the author is willing to treat the product like a business and work hard at selling the book. That means building a platform, perhaps through speaking or maintaining a website, to sell the book. It means creating a marketing plan and sticking with it. All book sale profits go directly to the author, a benefit to those out there selling lots of books. In fact, says Leal, she has made much more money selling her self published books than she has through earning royalties on other titles she has sold to traditional publishers.

Self publishing can also help an author build credibility. Book sales speak volumes to publishers looking for authors who know how to market. It also lets publishers know that an author has enough gumption to see a project through to the end.

Leal describes several negatives to self publishing. One is money. Costs can include paying for cover design, editing, printing, and marketing materials including mailings. It was a miracle, she says, that someone offered to pay printing costs for her first self-published book. She was able to repay the entire loan in nine months, plus donate over $10,000 to Huntington's disease research.

Another huge issue is distribution. Self-published books are very difficult to place in national chain bookstores because distribution channels are virtually nonexistent. Bookstores only order through a distributor, which rarely carries such books. Promises by self-publishing companies to put books into distribution channels often mean simply listing the title in a catalog containing many thousands of other books.

"What you don't have is a sales rep going into stores like Barnes & Noble or Family Christian and saying, 'This is a hot book,' so you won't get on the shelves," says Leal.

The third negative is time.

"It takes exhaustive, huge amounts of time to sell books and most people don't choose to do it. For whatever reason they cannot invest the time," she says.

Leal's book *How To Market Your Book* offers many alternative ways to sell books, but they are "grassroots ways," she says. And each one takes time.

Leal believes that her first self-published books gave her the initial credibility she needed when she proposed books to traditional, royalty publishers. *Writerspeaker.com: Internet Research and Marketing for Writers and Speakers* was published by Harold Shaw in 2000. She has also written *You Can Market Your Book: All the Tools You Need to Sell Your Published Book* (Write Now!, 2003). *The Twenty-Third Psalm for Caregivers* (AMG Publishers) is the first in a series that includes *The Twenty-Third Psalm for Those Who Grieve*.

"While I made so much more money from the self-published books, the traditionally published books gave me the most credibility."

She speaks at writers' conferences around the country and even attracted an agent, who signed Leal after reading *Writerspeaker.com*.

Leal and her husband currently live in Hawaii.

Reasons to Self Publish   The following reasons were distilled from Carmen Leal's website www.carmenleal.com/WS/Reasons.html, and are used by permission:

Time. I realized that people needed my book now, not in two or three or four years. The time to get a manuscript from my desk through the submission process and eventually into the hands of my readers was going to take longer than I wanted. I was able to write, edit, proofread, and release my book exactly one year after I started.

Control. In *Faces of Huntington's* I knew what I was trying to accomplish, but no one else did. I didn't want the risk of being told there was too much "God" in my book, or not enough medical jargon or speculation of a cure. I simply wanted to be able to control the content of the book.

Profit. Profit was of very little concern to me except I wanted to repay the non-interest loan that was given to me by a friend. I was able to do this in six months, and now all the profit can go to other Huntington's disease projects, or even to funding new books. I have control of where the money goes, and I'm not limited by the five-to-fifteen-percent royalty that is paid in the "business."

Possession. By using traditional, and even vanity, publishing houses, you no longer own your manuscript. You also have to purchase your own books to be able to give or sell them. If they lose interest in your book, you will not be able to print additional copies unless you purchase those rights back. Because I self published my book, I own exclusive rights.

Filling a niche. This was probably my number-one reason for writing the book. When my husband was diagnosed with Huntington's disease, I found little to read about the disease and less still about the people who were going through the same problems. Surprisingly, in self publishing, sometimes the more narrow your audience, the better. Books designed for the needs of a smaller audience may not be found in the mass market because publishers feel the demand is not great enough to warrant a large press run. I immediately became knowledgeable once I began caregiving, and I positioned myself as the expert with this book.

Locality. Books or newsletters about local or regional topics are usually produced by the author because of limited sales potential. That doesn't mean it isn't a good idea; it simply means the large overhead of a company doesn't make a short run about something local a possibility. These types of projects can often be sold in bulk to places like the Chamber of Commerce or specific businesses like real estate companies and banks.

Legacy. Sometimes sharing your knowledge and leaving a legacy to your family are enough to take the time and make the investment in a self published book. While that wasn't my reason for publishing *Faces of Huntington's*, I am proud to leave that as a legacy. My faith shines through the pages of this book, and my children will always know me through this and future projects.

Tips for Self Publishing   The following tips are used with permission from Carmen Leal (www.carmenleal.com/WS/tips.html):

- Study the competition.
- Write what other people want to read.
- Write where there is a void in the market.
- Think "marketing" from the very beginning.
- Get professional editing.
- Create a memorable, easy title.
- Have a fabulous cover. Four-color is preferable, but screens and tints can make a 2-color cover look like three colors or more at lower cost than four-color.
- Give attention to the inside pages. Make the book clean and easy to read.
- Use a book manufacturer for printing versus a local printer.
- Order extra covers at press time. The cost is minimal while the cover is on the press. Covers can be sent out as part of the press kit and for advertising. Also, print oversized postcards at the same time to use as direct mail pieces. Bookmarks and rack cards can be printed as well. You can print the copy on the preprinted cards later.
- Rather than send out review copies to every prospect, send out a book cover along with front matter, sample chapters, illustrations, charts, or other important book components. This is called a "blad."
- One word: Internet. You can create a home page to sell your book even before the book is in your hands. You may also offer free chapters of your book on-line, join electronic

mailing lists related to your topic, and link your book site to other related sites.

- Draw up a list of friends, family, business associates, and others who already have an interest in you and your work. Use those post cards you printed to announce the book.
- It's always a good idea to get more than one bid for your project.

Carmen Leal's websites:
www.thetwentythirdpsalm.com
www.carmenleal.com
www.writerspeaker.com
www.allaboutquotes.com

Chapter 11

Small Houses Take on Big Roles
Judith Markham

*"If you value good and consistent attention
from an editor and publisher,
a small house is worth considering."*

J udith Markham spent nineteen years at a major Christian publishing house. She started as an assistant editor, eventually becoming an acquiring editor with her own imprint.

She left the company to start Blue Water Ink, an editorial and
book packaging company, with two business associates.

In 2001 she joined Discovery House Publishers to fill in as managing editor when the man in that role was called up to active mili-
tary duty for a year after the September 2001 terrorist attacks. She
stayed on part time after he returned, moving to full time after he
took on a new role at RBC Ministries, parent company of Discovery
House Publishers.

Her role as managing editor at this small house includes working with the publisher, managing the house's complete list of books,
putting together each season's new list, sitting on the publishing
committee, and making some acquisitions. She occasionally edits
books, as well as sees them through the production process, which
includes cover design, interior design, and title.

"We're a small house but a very lively house," she says with a
laugh.

Markham has experienced and understands the pros and cons
of working with both a big publishing house and a small one.

The excitement of working with big-name authors, celebrities
and best-selling books is a huge plus to working at a big publishing house. Bigger houses also have the resources to do big things,
she says. Advances and marketing budgets are bigger, which means
more well known authors are drawn to the house.

"It's exciting to be part of something large and dynamic," she says. "It's exciting to acquire a book and have it become a household word."

The downside, says Markham, is that the pressure is intense for both employees and writers. Editors are under pressure to find bestsellers and get them out quickly, while authors are under pressure to write those bestsellers, for which they demand big advances.

With that pressure comes huge competition for those bestselling authors. One house sees the success of a particular book, then tries to woo that author to their own house. Not only authors bounce from house to house: editors do as well. The editor who acquired your book and has a passion for it may be replaced by someone who doesn't know your work, perhaps relegating it to the back burner.

"It can be frustrating for authors to get bounced around from editor to editor," says Markham.

Small publishing houses offer a number of benefits. For Markham it means being involved at all levels of the book, from acquisition to production. She does a variety of things instead of specializing in just one, as is the case in many big houses. It's also a slower pace. While deadlines loom every day, the stress level is much lower.

For authors, the benefits of working with a small house are many. For one thing, an agent isn't necessary. Discovery House rarely works with agents, is never barraged with manuscripts sent by agents, and even accepts unsolicited manuscripts.

"We're looking for good, well written, and biblically based material, but we don't care if somebody's a celebrity. In fact, that's not what we're looking for at all. To me that's a positive thing," says Markham.

The downside for authors is that Discovery House does not pay advances, and if they do it is not large. This isn't often a problem for the authors they publish, but it does tend to keep away celebrity authors looking for big bucks.

One of the greatest advantages of working with a small house is the individual attention each author receives. There are no A-list authors receiving the bulk of publicity dollars, no B- or C-list authors buried under the big names.

"When you do twelve books a year, all authors are treated equally," says Markham. "They all get pretty much the same kind of attention because the list is easier to manage."

Discovery House has a fantastic direct mail outlet via RBC Ministries, but they do struggle with finding shelf space in the bookstores. While Discovery House looks for well written books regardless of an author's platform, bookstores often want to know who the author is and whether his or her books will sell to a wide audience. Smaller publishers may mean lesser-known names, which means more difficulty getting on the shelves.

Small publishers are also good for books with a niche market tapped by that house. A book of poetry, for example, would be better served by a small house that does well with poetry than a big house that doesn't. That smaller house may also have better attention from bookstores that know the market and that publisher.

Markham urges authors to be realistic about a number of things:

1. Small houses often don't offer advances. Learn all you can about a publishing house so that you know what to expect from it.

2. You aren't the only author the editor works with, so he or she can't drop everything to call you back right away.

3. Small houses can offer more personal attention in editing and marketing, as well as equal shares of resources. Big houses often have more marketing clout, but you may not get any of it.

4. Smaller houses are just as eager for your book to do well as you are. They'll put their resources behind it.

5. Not everyone in the world will want to read your book, so don't expect huge sales and bunches of extravagant reviews.

BEST SELLER TIP **What's a Book Packager?**

Companies such as Blue Water Ink offer full-service book packaging to publishers or individuals. The packager takes a book through the production process, often doing editing, cover design, inside design, graphics, and print-ready services.

Publishers short on time and manpower often contact book packagers to bring a book to press for them. The publisher may take bids from several companies before making a choice or, depending on cost and resources available, contract for a portion of the packager's services.

"A book packager essentially puts the whole book together to take it off the editor's desk, which gives him or her more time to do something else," says Markham. "Every step of the way a packager will go back to the publisher for approval."

Some book packagers will work on self-published material, and most do not offer marketing services.

"If you value good and consistent attention from an editor and publisher, a small house is worth considering," says Markham. "You must look at what a publisher does well, study their lists, visit bookstores to see who does what, and then look beyond the first schmooze. Ask yourself what that company will do for you once they have you in the corral."

Jerry Jenkins
Terri Blackstock Lauren Winner
Karen Kingsbury
James Scott Bell Brandilyn Collins Angela Elwell Hunt Davis Bunn
Melody Carlson Sally Stuart Melody Carlson
Charlene Ann Baumbich Nancy Rue
Jack Cavanaugh
Barbara Nicolosi Justin Lookadoo
Dennis Hensley Dave Lambert & Lin Johnson

SECTION THREE

Meet the Pros: Dissecting the Christian Novel

Chapter 12

Jack Cavanaugh

DISSECTING THE
CHRISTIAN NOVEL
Jack Cavanaugh

*"If you want to write Christian fiction,
be a serious student of the craft.
If you love to read Christian fiction,
enjoy it now, but the best is yet to come."*

Jack Cavanaugh is author of more than twenty novels including the American Family Portrait series, the Songs in the Night series, *Death Watch* and *Dear Enemy*. He has won a Silver Medallion Award for *The Puritans* and two Christy Awards for excellence in Christian fiction for *While Mortals Sleep* and *His Watchful Eye*. He's coauthored several books and teaches at writers' conferences across the country. He definitely knows popular Christian fiction and how to write it. The key, Cavanaugh says, is knowing reader expectations. Those expectations are few but powerful.

Know Reader Expectations   **1. Readers expect to be introduced to the protagonist in the first chapter.** Cavanaugh tells the story of an author who lost the sale of his manuscript for this reason. The author had written the first chapter and populated it with emotion-charged characters in a dramatic setting. Those characters, however, weren't the protagonists, and when they were killed at the end of the chapter, the publisher was so disappointed that it rejected the book.

2. Readers want a strong plot. Readers won't tolerate a weak or implausible plot. The plot must work well, generate excitement, and keep readers interested.

3. Readers want a puzzle in novel form. "Readers love to figure out what's going to happen and are delighted when the author surprises them. They love the questions being raised, being led down blind alleys," says Cavanaugh. "As authors we must keep them on the edge of their seats; if readers have it all figured out, they're going to put the book down."

4. Readers want a great deal of action. Cavanaugh takes Hollywood producer Samuel Goldwyn's advice to heart: "Open with an earthquake and build from there." He also puts to good use what he gleaned from author Ken Follette, who makes sure change occurs often.

"It doesn't have to be a major change, but something has to change about the situation every four pages," says Cavanaugh.

At this point, beginning authors start to sweat. They're stammering about how their novel is about a small town like Mitford where earthquakes don't happen. They're writing a novel for young adults where the biggest thing is a blemish or a trip to the mall. They're writing about elderly people or a romance or historical fiction.

"Action, or a crisis, has to be defined in relationship to the character," says Cavanaugh. "You can have a teenage girl looking in the mirror and seeing a blemish and the prom is that night. That's an earthquake for her."

It's all about introducing the protagonist, then creating an earthquake in that person's life of whatever size is appropriate. Change, great or small, must come often.

5. Readers want colorful and convincing characters. Readers want people they can love and people they can hate, from the main character to the lesser knowns.

"As fiction writers we need to get better at developing characters," says Cavanaugh. "But, the bottom line is that as Christians we need to be working to write the best fiction the world has ever seen."

The Future of Christian Fiction Cavanaugh himself says he's ten years away from doing his best work. He promoted himself from apprentice to journeyman two novels ago. As for Christian fiction, it's still in its infancy in this rebirth of the genre.

"Keep supporting Christian fiction, but hang in there and give us ten, fifteen, twenty more years. Then you're going to see some really, really good stuff," he says.

Every writer from beginner to master can work on improving his or her craft. It's nothing new, according to Cavanaugh. Just read and read some more, and write and write some more. He urges writers to read contemporary novels, but also great works of the faith from generations past. His list includes *The Shepherd of Hermas*, Dante's *Divine Comedy*, *Pilgrim's Progress* by Bunyan, *Paradise Lost* and *Paradise Regained* by Milton, *The Lord of the Rings* by Tolkein, *The Chronicles of Narnia* by Lewis, *In His Steps* by Charles Sheldon, and *Magnificent Obsession* by Lloyd C. Douglas.

"Our goal as Christian writers should be to have our books still in print several generations from now," says Cavanaugh, "so we need to read, read, read and write, write, write. Write every day. I mean, write! Researching is not writing. Going to a writers' conference is not writing. Reading about writing is not writing. Talking about writing is not writing. There is no substitute for putting words on a page.

BEST SELLER TIP: Two Can Be Better Than One

Jack Cavanaugh has coauthored books with Bill Bright, who was president of Campus Crusade for Christ, and Jerry Kuiper, founder of Save a Friend Ministries. Each coauthoring relationship was different, and each process was different.

The bottom line is that the relationships have to be beneficial to both authors. Cavanaugh's writing expertise put flesh to Dr. Bright's ideas for a series on revivals in American history. Jerry Kuiper's idea helped Cavanaugh achieve his goal of writing contemporary suspense.

The marketing expertise of Kuiper and the public relations muscle of Dr. Bright's organization can only help Cavanaugh.

"Both coauthors need to bring something to the table," he says.

"I teach young writers the things I learned and the mistakes I've made and we've all made over the last ten to fifteen years. We're training a new generation of writers who have better opportunities because they're getting started on the right foot and not having to feel their way. We have the possibility of raising a new generation of writers who can really produce some great material," he says.

Chapter 13

Charlene Ann Baumbich

WRITING AS LISTENING
Charlene Ann Baumbich

*"Writing is quiet for me because I'm listening.
I'm writing what I'm hearing.
Writing is very prayerful to me.
I am open to hear everything."*

Nobody ever calls Charlene Baumbich shy, retiring, quiet, or meek. She's more like a belly laugh, a constant stream of rapid-fire talk, hilarity, and storytelling. When it comes to writing, however, Baumbich is a listener.

She listens to the stories that want to be heard. She listens to characters who want to be known. In fact, several characters in her popular Dearest Dorothy series introduced themselves to her in a surprising way.

An editor from Guidepost Books called Baumbich one day to ask if she had any ideas for senior citizen characters. Baumbich had recently lost her father and two other older people in her life, including the real Dearest Dorothy, so older folks were heavy on her mind. She wasn't thinking about writing fiction, hadn't talked to anyone about it. She figured the editor was brainstorming characters for a novelist. But when she called that editor back with ideas for characters, something changed.

"I was suddenly proprietary about these characters. The editor asked me to tell her about them, so I did. While I was talking, the fictional Dorothy walked up behind the real Dorothy I was picturing and stepped right through her and stood in front of me. This character started growing on her own. Then another character stepped up beside her. His name is Arthur Landers and he's this

Books by Charlene Baumbich

Don't Miss Your Kids! (They'll be gone before you know it!) (InterVarsity Press)

How to Eat Humble Pie & Not Get Indigestion (InterVarsity Press)

Mama Said There'd Be Days Like This (but she never said just how many) (Vine Books)

The Book of Duh (Shaw Books)

365 Ways to Connect with Your Kids (Career Press)

The 12 Dazes of Christmas (& One Holy Night) (InterVarsity Press)

Dearest Dorothy, Bk. 1: Are We There Yet? (Penguin)

Dearest Dorothy, Bk. 2: Slow Down, You're Wearing Us Out (Penguin Books)

Dearest Dorothy, Bk. 3: Help! I've Lost Myself! (Penguin Books)

Dearest Dorothy, Bk. 4: Who Would Have Ever Thought?!

crotchety old guy who is a good friend of Dorothy's and who works on her car. That's it; there they were," she marvels.

The editor asked her to write up descriptions of these characters, then called back several days later to ask Baumbich what she thought the characters might be doing.

"I squinted my eyes and started talking about what I saw in my head: about a setting, a town, a place," Baumbich says. "She asked me to write up little descriptions of what might be in a book. I said, 'Well, that's a little hard to do because there isn't a book.'"

Baumbich did it anyway; then the editor called again and wanted her to write something about a second book.

"I said, 'There is no book one. How can I possibly know what will be happening in book two?' She told me to use my imagination because I'm good at that."

Those characters who stepped into Baumbich's imagination were the genesis of the Dearest Dorothy series. It began as a two-book series for Guidepost Books, which sold 35,000 sets via mail order and the Internet. Penguin Books editor Carolyn Carlson saw them, loved them, and immediately licensed the pair from Guidepost Books. They were repackaged and released into bookstores in 2004, and Baumbich signed contracts with Penguin for books three through five.

"I feel like I'm flying when I'm writing. It's so exhilarating. When I'm watching a story run in my head I don't feel like an author. I feel like a recorder," she says. "My job is to type as fast as I can to not miss any of it, to get it all down."

For a woman who loves to talk and laugh, listening is key to her writing.

"Writing is quiet for me because I'm listening. I'm writing what I'm hearing. Writing is very prayerful to me. I am open to hearing everything," she says.

The story, however, does involve work. She laughs when she says the work of the story involves biting her nails down to nubs, but she's serious when she says that story comes from life.

"How can you write about life if you're not living it? I have to do a lot of lunches with people, even when I'm holed up writing," she says.

There's the work of travel to promote her books and the travel due to her active speaking schedule. She speaks often at women's Christian ministry events on the subject of "Don't Miss Your Life." It's a platform, she says, that is beneficial for sales of both her non-fiction books and her novels. But most importantly, speaking enables her to express her passions directly to people thirsting to be reminded that life is good. *Don't Miss Your Life! It's Better Than You Think* (Penguin Books, 2007) resulted from Baumbich's speaking engagements.

Baumbich's readers can always get a regular dose of her wit and wisdom through her TwinkleGrams, sent free via e-mail. Baumbich has never hidden her faith or the faith of her characters in the Dearest Dorothy series. Her secular publisher and her many readers never seem to mind.

"What delights me is that I've got a character who not only is a woman of faith but who cites Bible chapter and verse. People not looking for Christian fiction are finding this feisty woman who isn't afraid to give God a little what-for and to pray about everything," she says.

"The key point is to honor the story, and when you do that the story offers its own message for readers. People tell me incredible things about how a character spoke to them. It's the marvelous, magical, awesome, dripping, oozing work of the Holy Spirit."

Baumbich suggests these ways to begin really listening to your characters.

1. Get out of your characters' way. Stop saying "I have to think of something clever for this character to say." The characters talk on their own, so zip your mental lips, quit trying to wordsmith, and just record what you "hear."

2. Relax. Stop telling yourself that writing is hard, and let your curiosity take over.

3. Pretend. Make believe you are a 5-year-old telling a whopper of a story only you can see in your head.

Find Charlene Ann Baumbich on the web at www.don'tmissyourlife. com and www.dearestdorothy.com. Get her free TwinkleGrams at www.twinklegram.com.

Chapter 14

Angela Elwell Hunt

IDEAS, REVISION, CRAFT, AND NAME RECOGNITION

Angela Elwell Hunt

"I don't want to write stories that don't thrill me. That boredom would bleed through to the reader."

A ngela Elwell Hunt can't remember how many books she's written. It's somewhere around a hundred, she says with a laugh. She's written picture books (*The True Princess* was recently rereleased by CharismaKids!), fiction and nonfiction for middle grade readers, parenting and family books, historical novels, contemporary fiction, and prophetic novels.

She answers questions about her life as a writer.

Question: *How did you come to write so many books in such a variety of genres?*

Angela: There was never a grand plan. I wrote books according to where I was. I wrote picture books when my children were young, middle-grade books because my husband is a youth pastor and I love kids, historical fiction because it was popular when my publisher asked me to try adult fiction. According to conventional wisdom, this was exactly the wrong thing to do. Conventional wisdom says to find a niche and write in that niche. That's why I've written a hundred books and few people have ever heard of me. But I see the hand of God through it all, and I have learned something from every step I've taken.

Question: *Where do your ideas come from?*

Angela: Ideas come from everywhere. Sometimes it's a setting. One time I read something about the rain forest and thought it would make a great setting for a book. I carried that idea around for more than two years.

Sometimes it's a concept, like the idea of the woman with a sordid past pouring oil on Jesus's feet. That became *The Debt*, about the wife of a televangelist who had been a hooker and had given up a child for adoption. Sometimes it's a character. Weird diseases fascinate me, as do unusual places and stories in the newspaper.

Question: *What do you do with all these ideas?*

Angela: I call it back-burnering. I have an idea file that I stick my ideas in and let them sit there. If I don't remember I put the idea there, the idea is dead. If the idea doesn't resonate when I pull it out a year or two later, it's no good. Sometimes I think something is a cool idea one day, but two days later think it's stupid. So the ideas that stick with me for a long period of time are the ones that I know have legs.

Most of the time I have a couple of ideas in my brain that I think someday I might use. Rarely does an idea pop to the forefront and demand to be written immediately. It has happened a couple of times, and on those occasions I think it was the voice of the Lord urging me to write something. *The Debt* was one of those.

Question: *How do you choose what to write?*

Angela: Everybody always says to write your passion, but it's said so often we don't pay attention. But when you get hold of that passionate idea that burns a hole in your heart, that's the thing you have to write then and there. I don't want to write stories that don't thrill me. That boredom would bleed through to the reader. Besides, I don't think I could stick with a boring story because the process of writing is too hard to invest months of your life in a story you don't like.

Question: *For you, what is most difficult about writing?*

Angela: It's all difficult, but for me, sitting in front of a blank screen and getting started is the hardest part. I am seized by insecurity. I'm seized by the fear that this idea that burns so brightly in my heart isn't going to translate properly onto the page.

I've often compared putting out a first draft to birthing a baby. You have to push it out; you cannot give up. But when it's sitting on the desk and it's all messy and slimy, it's a living thing and you go back and clean it up. The important thing is to go through the labor and push that first draft out.

Question: *Do you revise as you write that first draft?*

Angela: I try not to. When I teach, I always tell writers that they mustn't stop and polish. 'Push on, push on, push on,' I say. Because revision is a never-ending process. It will never be perfect, so get the story down. Then you can go back and clean up the baby.

Question: *What do you do once that first draft is done?*

Angela: I do what I call triage. When wounded soldiers come off the battlefield, the medical corps work on the most desperately wounded first. So I do triage on my manuscript. I ask myself what is missing, which characters are half formed, what needs to be rewritten, where are the holes? There are a lot of holes in a first draft because I don't know my characters well until I have seen the end of the story.

Sometimes I type in notes like "Research this" and "This is really stinky. Fix it!" But I don't stop. I know there are days when anything I write is going to be stinky. So I try to keep going.

Question: *How much rewriting have you had to do?*

Angela: I handed in a manuscript once, which I thought had moments of sheer brilliance … and my two editors hated it. That was the first time I heard the words, "We can't publish this as it is." I didn't cry; I think I was a little numb. But I read the editors' comments and realized they were right—my grand intellectual experiment had flopped. I did a complete rewrite. I threw out half the book and added another story, plus rewrote the part I kept. The book is called *The Novelist* and was released in 2006.

Question: *How do you deal with having to rewrite or revise your books?*

Angela: I have to trust my vision, but at the same time I have to trust my editors. They are professionals. They know what works; they love and respect me, but at the same time they want me to succeed as much as I do. I trusted my editors with *The Novelist* and they were absolutely right.

Question: *How do you build the characters in your books?*

Angela: I use the Myers-Briggs personality assessment test. Whenever I sit down to write a character, I ask myself the four definitive Myers-Briggs questions. As soon as I have answered those four questions, I have a character's personality type. I use one of the five or six Myers-Briggs books I have on my shelf, look up that personality type, and the book will tell me everything about that character's personality: what kind of car or house they have, what kind of clothes they wear, their strengths and weaknesses.

The characters are pretty fleshed out in my brain, but I go online to a site like www.tonystone.com and search through the images and find the one that looks like the character I'm creating. I download the picture, print it out, and tape it to the edge of my desk so that I can look at these people as I write.

Question: *Do you build plot or characters first?*

Angela: A lot of writers are more character oriented, but for me plot usually comes first. I usually do a very rough plot outline and then do scene cards. I write each scene on an index card. I do the first draft on note cards, then write the first draft. I do the same thing for the second and third drafts. I don't do the whole thing in one fell swoop because a story in progress is a very fluid thing. The story might take off in a direction I didn't expect.

Question: *What's your best piece of advice for beginning writers?*

Angela: Don't be in a hurry to get published; writing is a learning process. I started writing in 1983; for five years I wrote catalog copy, brochures, magazines articles, and anything else people would pay me to write. I never thought I'd write a book, never planned it, never dreamed it. Those years were my boot camp. Then I entered a contest and won a publishing contract.

I get e-mails all the time from people so desperate to get published that they want to go with a vanity press. I always advise against that because, if you publish something that's not up to par, the experience will do nothing to add to your credibility. It's much better to keep that manuscript in a drawer and consider it a learning experience. If it's rejected by a traditional publisher, it's probably not ready to market. So learn from it and keep going. In a few years, you may want to rewrite it.

Question: *Anything else?*

Angela: Write other things. If you want to be a novelist, hone your skills by writing for your denominational magazine or your church newsletter or whatever. Just write because, in writing, you learn.

Also, don't think your idea is the most precious thing in the world. Ideas are a dime a dozen and you can be sure somebody else has had the same idea you have. The idea isn't what matters. What matters to an editor is how you express that idea.

Part of this is to not copy what's already out there. One more thing: Don't copy the writers you admire. The world already has a Jerry Jenkins and a Francine Rivers; what it lacks is *you*.

Question: *What do you do to market your books?*

Angela: I do quiet things like my website, which I try to make as interesting as possible. I also do telephone discussions with book clubs that are using my books. It's my pleasure to call and chat with readers. I respond to e-mails and letters from people. I also try to send out a regular newsletter to my e-mail reader list and postcards about new releases to my snail mail reader list.

But mainly I try to be kind and treat people the way I'd like to be treated.

I discovered a long time ago that I can either concentrate on marketing or concentrate on writing. I don't have the time and patience to do both, so I do what I can through my website and correspondence and let my publisher handle the rest. I would rather concentrate on writing an irresistible story and trust the Lord to put my books in the hands where they belong than to run around like a headless chicken trying to push my books on people.

Question: *What do you expect from your publisher as far as marketing?*

Angela: I depend on my publisher to get my book into the stores, which means it needs to be in the catalog and have good back cover copy. My publisher sends me the back cover copy to approve, and at times I've even written the copy. You know your book better than anybody at the publishing house. I try to do everything I can comfortably do, then trust my publisher to do the rest.

Question: *What about book signings and travel?*

Angela: I never travel to promote my stuff, but I do travel to teach at writers' conferences. It's very rare that I do a book signing unless my publisher sets it up. If they ask me to do a signing I usually agree, but I don't set them up myself because I've done too many signings where I just sat and smiled.

Question: *How have you matured as a writer over the past ten years?*

Angela: I think I've become more outspoken about a lot of things. I'm dealing with heavier topics, even some that might be controversial. When I hit age forty-five I realized I was halfway to ninety and I thought, "I don't have time to piddle around writing weak stories." I want every book to have a message, to be scripturally sound.

I've also become a much tighter writer. WestBow is going to rerelease a novel I wrote in 1991, so I went back to the document file and started cutting unnecessary words. I think I cut 10,000

Did You Know?

Angie Hunt has written more than 100 books.

Sales top 1 million for *The Tale of Three Trees*.

Three Trees has been translated into nearly twenty languages.

She visited a rain forest to research a book.

She's written about pretzels, gorillas, and ancient Egypt.

words that didn't have to be there. As you write, you learn that tight is better. Another thing I've been doing lately is adding discussion questions or interview to the back of my books. I also don't want people to misinterpret my message, because sometimes it's subtle. Book group questions help point people to the truth of Christ—as well as sparking a good discussion!

Question: *Where would you like to be in five or ten years?*

Angela: I would love to be doing exactly what I'm doing now ... except writing about even wilder things.

Question: *What is one of your favorite things about writing books?*

Angela: I love hearing that one of my books touched someone's life. Nine times out of ten, when I hear that I know the touch came through the Holy Spirit, not through something I wrote. Readers tell me that a certain scene or phrase affected them, but I know it's the Spirit. I could never have intentionally planned that kind of effect.

Resources:
www.angelaelwellhunt.com
www.tonystone.com

For information on the Myers-Briggs Type Indicator testing, visit www.discoveryourpersonality.com

Chapter 15

Following God
in Christian Fiction
Terri Blackstock

*"Whenever I read a really great book
it makes me a better writer. ...
If I feel like I'm getting blocked or
my writing is kind of dry,
I read a great book that puts me into that cadence,
that rhythm I need to write more creatively."*

The best piece of writing advice Terri Blackstock ever heard is "Don't get it right; get it written." The worst advice she's heard is "Promote, promote, promote." In twenty years of writing she's learned to know what advice to take to heart and how to ignore the rest.

"I went to a writing seminar years ago and another writer encouraged us to write the whole first draft without editing. It was like a light came on because, until that point, I would write three chapters over and over trying to perfect them," says Blackstock. "I would lose interest, never getting past Chapter 3. Then I'd start a new book."

It was an issue of self-judgment. She wanted those chapters to be perfect before she went on, but soon realized that perfection would never come.

"What I needed was to build up my momentum and write the first draft all the way through as fast as I could, then go back and rewrite and rewrite and rewrite."

Blackstock is author of nearly thirty novels. She's written the Seasons series with Beverly LaHaye, the Cape Refuge, Newpointe 911 and Second Chances series and many other novels. Her career began, however, with romance novels for popular lines such as Silhouette. Book sales totaled about 3.5 million, and she was selling everything she wrote. But her faith was lukewarm; she began adding content to her romances that made for big sales but not for a strong testimony. During this time she went through a divorce and eventually remarried.

"I felt the Lord dealing with me. I felt like I had strayed so far from where he wanted me, that he had given me a gift and I had squandered it. Then about a year into my second marriage my husband had a spiritual awakening," says Blackstock.

His change of heart and life affected Blackstock as well. She longed to be used as her husband was, but knew that the type of books she wrote would hinder her testimony. After much prayer and a huge step of faith, Blackstock gave up writing romance novels and turned to writing Christian suspense novels. She wrote two proposals, found a Christian agent, and prepared to wait. But her novels sold immediately, thus launching her career in Christian fiction. Blackstock's books consistently sell well and her fan base grows with each one. Zondervan releases one of her books about every nine months, with no end in sight.

Reading is the Best Break   Blackstock must move quickly from project to project to meet reader demand and honor contract obligations. Despite the volume of work she does, Blackstock takes time between projects to regroup. Her favorite downtime activity is reading good books.

"Whenever I read a really great book it makes me a better writer," she says. "Books really inspire me. If I feel like I'm getting blocked or my writing is kind of dry, I read a great book that puts me into that cadence, that rhythm I need to write more creatively."

Part of the creative writing process is building a great plot. Blackstock uses what she calls "storyboard plotting."

"A number of years ago I did a book about an animator. As I started researching what animators do, I saw that they use a storyboard system for plotting their cartoons. I thought it would work great for novels. I got a bulletin board and index cards and plotted out every scene that I could," she says.

These days she plots her novels on the computer, creating a table that includes chapter number, point of view, what day the scene takes place, what time of day, and the scene itself. She figures she plots about 100 pages at time, something she learned from screenwriting.

"In a screenplay you have three acts. The first act is one-fourth of the movie, the second act is half, and the third act is the last fourth.

I divide my project into those four parts," says Blackstock. "I plot about one-fourth of the book at a time and usually at the end of that fourth there is something that changes the plot in some way."

She writes to catch up with her plotting, often knowing in general what will happen next, but waiting to plot out the next section until the writing catches up. Pieces of the plot may change, of course, in what she calls a revolving outline.

"I write the first draft as quickly as I can without much judgment and without worrying about being really creative in everything. Then on the second draft I start getting more creative, and at that point I may change my outline. In each of the drafts I can change the plot pretty drastically," says Blackstock.

Plot changes come when she feels something isn't working quite right or her editor suggests something needs to be clearer or flow better or make better sense. Sometimes she knows what needs tweaking, other times her editor's suggestions reveal the problems. Rarely does she ignore the editor's advice.

"When I don't take their advice it's usually because I don't think their answer is going to work any better," she says. "But I'll realize there is a problem and will figure something else out."

Freelance editor Dave Lambert edits Blackstock's work at her request, despite the sometimes lengthy critiques she receives from him.

"He will write pages and pages and pages of critique. Most people hate that, but I absolutely love it because where else would you get that thorough a critique of your book?" she says.

Not that she embraces those critiques the minute she gets one.

"Frankly, I can't read them the first day I get one of those revision letters. I'll just count the pages and see how much stuff is there. A couple of days later I will kind of read part of it. I have to ease into it," she says with a laugh. "It does require giving up my ego, but I'm painfully aware of my shortcomings as a writer and realize that every one of those suggestions is usually going to help improve the book."

Advice for Writers   That's one of Blackstock's key pieces of advice to writers: Take that critique and learn from it. Be wary, however, of critique from an acquaintance who might rip a manuscript to shreds out of jealousy.

"But when you're getting advice from a professional editor, you know you can trust him, because he's not out to get you but to make the book better," says Blackstock. "It's really important to seek out great editors."

Blackstock says it's also important to be in a writer's group with others on your level who are as committed to writing as you are. She belongs to an online group that allows her to get to know other writers, ask research questions, and hold each other accountable. The group is currently doing a study of systematic theology in an effort to help each other clarify what they believe and why they believe it.

She also suggests attending writers' conferences to meet other writers, make contacts with editors, and learn the craft.

"I have never been to a conference that was a waste of time," she says.

A final suggestion is to just read. Read novels in your genre as well as outside it, looking at the language and style to help hone your own craft.

Igniting the Creative Spark Blackstock has contracts for a number of books with Zondervan. The ideas came to her, then she wrote a plot synopsis that resulted in a contract. The ideas, she says, come from everywhere: an overheard conversation, a talk with a friend or acquaintance, or her own imagination.

"I believe God gives me all these wonderful ideas. I think he gave me a fertile imagination so that I can see these ideas and flesh them out pretty quickly. He also gives me insight as I'm writing on things I hope will linger in the minds of the readers and maybe cause a change in their lives," says Blackstock.

She starts most days with Bible study, which centers her, and prayer that calms and focuses. She can usually tell when she doesn't spend time with God.

"I'm not as creative and I'm not as focused. I tend to spin my wheels a lot more," she says. "God is very active in the writing of my books."

Blackstock made a conscious decision to make God part of her work, which is reflected in her mission statement. Her mission, she says, is to lead people back to the Bible and to challenge readers to bear more fruit in their lives.

"As Christian writers, we all have a purpose in our writing, something we'd like to do with it. It may be to just entertain with clean fiction, and that's valid. It's important for us to get that in our minds so that we don't get off course, maybe take on a bunch of projects that don't live up to our mission statement."

Blackstock says no to projects all the time. Every time a publisher approaches her about a collaborative project or some other thing, she runs it through her mission statement grid. If it doesn't fit, she says no. As she's gained success, she's had to say no much more often. She often says no to other writers' requests for endorsements and to speaking engagements, both of which take time and energy away from her writing.

Despite having to say no to many projects, Blackstock finds much joy in writing. One of her greatest joys is hearing from readers whose lives have been changed through her books. Readers have accepted Christ through her work, as well as renewed their relationships with God.

"I've gotten letters from people saying, 'I'm not going to read any more of your novels because you've convicted me that I need to be reading my Bible.' I consider that a success," she laughs.

It's also a joy to get new covers to look over. It's fun, she says, to see a book take shape—to see it as readers will—as well as see it on the bookshelves once it's released.

The difficulties, she says, come not from being a Christian writer specifically but from being a writer in general. Some days she doesn't feel like writing; other days there are many distractions. Often it's difficult to leave her writing and interact with her family. She calls it getting the right balance between real life and fictional life. It's real life, she says, that provides her with things to write about. There are also times when she compares herself to other writers who sell more or are doing more promotion.

The comparison hearkens back to that advice to "promote, promote, promote." She does what she can, which isn't much compared to some authors. But that's fine, she says.

"I know a lot of writers who invest lots of money into promotional materials and things they think are helping sell the book, or they take lots of speaking engagements. I found out pretty early that that wasn't a good use of my time," she says.

There's also an issue of stewardship. God gives you a book, a publisher, and an audience. What is the best use of that book and your time? Is purchasing lots of promotional material a good use of money? Is traveling a long way to a book signing, only to have three people show up, a good use of time? Is it worth time away from family?

"I've heard people stand up and talk about what they do for marketing and how they promote their book, and it just exhausts me. I compare myself to them and think I should be doing more, but my husband reminds me of my mission statement. All that promotion is not what God has called me to do."

Blackstock does speak at writers' conferences, which she feels is a good use of time because she's giving back to the writing community. She limits those, though, because she's got a child still at home and because it takes away from writing time.

"I learned so much from writers who went before me, so it's fun to show other writers some of the techniques that work for me," she says.

The bottom line for Blackstock is writing. She tailors her day and her time to writing, avoiding projects or commitments that take away from that. She does only what promotion she can.

"Really, the best promotion is to write a great book."

For more information on Terri Blackstock and her books, visit www.terriblackstock.com.

Chapter 16

James Scott Bell
THE LEARNING NEVER STOPS
James Scott Bell

*"The fundamental, unalterable rule is that
you must understand writing is a craft."*

James Scott Bell didn't start out a successful, full-time writer. He dreamed of being one, but a steady paycheck seemed like a good thing so he went to law school and became a lawyer. But that writing dream kept niggling his brain, so Bell took the first step toward reaching his new career goal.

He began studying screenwriting, or at least restudying it. He'd taken classes during college as well as studied acting, but Bell recognized that the learning curve was looming for him. He learned, wrote, learned some more, and wrote some more.

He had some success, nothing that made it to the Big Screen he's quick to say, then decided to write something by himself after the ultracollaborative work of screenwriting. Another stop on the learning curve had him studying how to write a novel.

"I wrote this very crazy, wacky novel called *The Darwin Conspiracy*. I was convinced no one would publish it, but it ended up that somebody did and I said 'Okay!' and that's how I got started," says Bell.

It was his career as a lawyer that provided the next step. Bell began writing Christian legal thrillers and ended up with a 5-book contract with Broadman & Holman. Now Bell has written more than a dozen novels, plus nonfiction books for trial lawyers and the popular *Plot and Structure*, and is the fiction columnist for *Writer's Digest* magazine.

He's learned valuable lessons along the way.

Big Screen to Published Book — From screenwriting he learned the importance of getting into the opening scene quickly and immediately establishing some conflict or tension.

"I always counsel new writers not to warm up their engines but to get something happening from the first page," says Bell. "It's important, too, because an editor or agent is going to be your first reader."

It's not your clear, concise, and meaty cover letter that attracts them. It's not your provocative plot synopsis they turn to first. It's your first chapter.

"Agents and editors figure if the person can't write or if the story isn't moving, they'll know by the first chapter and then not have to waste time on the whole proposal," says Bell.

A great lead is absolutely crucial, whether it's character-driven for a novel or a hook that draws readers into a nonfiction book or newspaper or magazine article. In novels it must include the main character.

Novel leads come in several forms: the traditional hero, or positive lead; the antihero who operates under his own code; and the negative lead, a difficult but not impossible task for the writer.

Bell also learned how to write crisp dialogue. Because a screenplay is mostly dialogue, he learned not to waste time.

"The secret of great dialogue is not to recreate real-life speech, but to write purposeful speech that sounds like it's real life," says Bell. "There is always a purpose to everything you write. With dialogue you want to make sure there is some kind of conflict or tension or subtext that's going on beneath the speech."

Bell has also learned to let his plot and characters evolve. There are certain elements that he locks in: the direction of the story, how he wants it to come out, what the lead character really wants, and what's trying to stop him or her. This allows him to think through the book, filling in as he goes.

"My characters usually evolve as I'm writing. That's purposeful in one sense because I want the story to develop and characters to interact and be able to go in a different direction if necessary," says Bell. "I try to create interesting characters at the beginning, characters I want to spend time with and then watch as they grow."

As for plot, he doesn't map out the entire story. "I have scene ideas, but the story is always going to be organic. It's going to take on a life of its own. I want to allow it that breathing space."

Can a character change the plot? It may change some of the twists on the way, but Bell still knows where the story will end up. Isn't that scary? No. Bell knows the main character and his opposition, so scenes won't be that far afield.

The Bell Curve   Bell is a writing teacher along with his roles as novelist and columnist. He speaks often at writers' conferences, encouraging beginning writers to not believe what he calls the Big Lie. Yes, he says, you can learn to write. Writing isn't a secret society, a novel isn't drawn from a dark place in the soul, an article doesn't spring forth in a fit of creativity given only to a few.

The first step in learning to write is a real desire, "a compulsion to want to write," and an understanding that it takes a long time to both learn and practice.

Bell himself sets aside at least two hours a week to read or reread books on the craft of writing. He knows that a writer is never done learning.

"In any other profession, the law for example, you have to keep up on it. You have to read the latest cases, take continuing education courses. Why would it be any different as a professional writer?" Bell asks. "You can't just read about writing and then think you're a great writer. You have to constantly be practicing and interacting with books and with classes and with good teachers. So it's a combination of writing constantly, daily if possible, and constantly learning."

Bell also encourages beginning writers to attend a writers' conference to link up with others writers and those in the publishing business, as well as to join a critique group.

"The fundamental, unalterable rule is that you must understand writing is a craft," he says. "Just because you care passionately about a story or you feel moved to write it or because it really happened to your grandmother, if you cannot craft it in a way that will make readers respond, none of those things matter."

For established writers, Bell encourages setting a weekly word quota. Set the quota, then divide by the number of days you are writing. If one day lags, try to make up for it another day. He also urges writers to complete whatever writing project they're working on. Completing a novel or nonfiction book or article, whether it gets published or not, is a learning process.

"If you do that regularly, week after week and year after year, you are going to be a very prolific, productive writer," he says.

Priority Assessment   Jim Bell puts learning the writing craft at the top of his professional priority list. On top of his spiritual priority list is time alone with God. He schedules time with God, reads Scripture nearly every day, and spends time in prayer.

"It's possible to become a published writer and allow your spiritual life to languish, to make your career the center of your life. You can get caught up in all the promotion and stuff that goes along with being a published writer. You have to work really hard to remain centered on God and not on yourself or your career," says Bell.

When he senses his priorities getting out of whack, he gets away from the office and the deadlines to be alone with God. He usually takes Sundays off to allow himself a Sabbath rest. Bell's goal is to weave his faith into his work naturally.

"I think from the start God has given me the ability to write for a nonbelieving reader as well as believers. I feel like I'm able to communicate the faith aspect of my life through the book. The books, therefore, are not preaching and not sermons."

Christian fiction twenty years ago, says Bell, was just an excuse for characters to mouth Christian slogans or preach a sermon. It's come a long way in the last two decades, with the future looking even brighter. More and better writers are going to draw a bigger nonbelieving audience looking for hope and for stories that "don't drag them through the mud in a bad way.

"It's not that Christian fiction avoids the hard issues, because it's now taking on virtually everything. But it's offering that hope, that answer I think is the deepest yearning of people out there. As the quality of Christian fiction improves, people in the world are going to start hearing about it," Bell says.

Writing Hints from Jim Bell: **1. Get those first pages of a novel moving.** It doesn't have to be physical action, but there must be some tension, some challenge to the lead character.

2. Research is vital. Bell uses the library to research historical novels and finds sources to help him get the facts, moods, and insider stuff correct in current-day novels.

3. God is in the details. Bell takes an insight from Stephen King to heart: People like to read about the details of a character's professional life. Bell makes sure to include such details.

4. Grab on to coattails when you can. This worked for Bell. He coauthored *The Shannon Saga* with Tracie Peterson. This was a calculated plan by Bethany House Publishers to introduce Bell to their audience through his work with a well known Bethany author. He now writes successful novels for the publisher under his name alone.

5. Keep an idea file. Bell writes down one or two-line ideas gleaned from his reading or his imagination, files them, and occasionally goes through the file looking for something to develop further. He's never run out of ideas for his *Writer's Digest* fiction column. "The craft of writing is so wide and vast that there is always something else you can dig into. I enjoy picking up new things in my own writing and reading. I enjoy writing about the craft."

6. Make it good. Bell strives to send the best draft possible to his editor, though he concedes that an established author could submit a partial manuscript if he or she is having trouble with it.

7. Work *with* your editor. It's important to understand that the editor is there to help you, not persecute you. The editor isn't always right, so Bell has been known to take a stand on issues. He also understands an editor is offering a suggestion, so considering that suggestion is worthwhile.

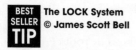 **The LOCK System**
© James Scott Bell

L is for **Lead**
The point here is that a strong plot starts with an interesting lead character. In the best plots, that lead is compelling, someone we have to watch throughout the course of the novel. This does not mean the lead has to be entirely sympathetic.

O is for **Objective**
Objective is the driving force of fiction. It generates forward motion and keeps the lead from just sitting around. An objective can take either of two forms: to get something or to get *away* from something. Solid plots have one and only one dominant objective for the lead character.

C is for **Confrontation**
Opposition from characters and outside forces brings your story fully to life. If your lead moves toward his objective without anything in his way, we deprive readers of what they secretly want: worry. Readers want to fret about the lead, keeping an intense emotional involvement all the way through the novel. Make things tough on your lead. Never let him or her off easy.

K is for **Knockout**
Readers want to see a knockout at the end. A great ending can leave the reader satisfied, even if the rest of the book is somewhat weak. But a weak ending will leave the reader with a feeling of disappointment, even if the book up to that point is strong. So take your lead through the journey toward his or her objective, and then send the opposition to the mat.

This version of Bell's LOCK system was condensed from Chapter 1 of *Plot and Structure* (Writer's Digest Books).

A discussion of the LOCK system is also available on Bell's website: www.jamesscottbell.com.

Jerry Jenkins
Terri Blackstock Lauren Winner
Karen Kingsbury
James Scott Bell Brandilyn Collins Angela Elwell Hunt Davis Bunn
Melody Carlson Sally Stuart Melody Carlson
Charlene Ann Baumbich
Jack Cavanaugh Nancy Rue
Barbara Nicolosi Justin Lookadoo
Dennis Hensley Dave Lambert & Lin Johnson

Know the Kids: Tapping into the Children's, Tween, and Young Adult Markets

Chapter 17

Melody Carlson

TEEN HEARTBEAT

Melody Carlson

*"It's a tightrope walk to have the book be real
and talk the way teens talk without being
out of date too soon. You want to sound timely
but you don't want to sound goofy."*

M elody Carlson calls her writing journey "unplanned" by human standards but thoroughly planned by God. Despite loving to write as a high school and college student, it wasn't until her sons were becoming teenagers that she felt the compulsion to write.

"We were going to the general bookstores, and I was seeing the horrible stuff that was available back in the mid-1990s. There wasn't much in Christian bookstores either. I started writing short stories and actually had one published within that first year," says Carlson.

Several years later, after working her way up to children's editor at Multnomah Publishers in Sisters, Oregon, and juggling her growing writing career, she left her job to become a fulltime writer.

"I figured I would just quietly work at Multnomah, then come home and write and play with my boys, get them through high school and college. But God really did have a plan. My writing just took off," she says. "It had always been my desire to write, but I didn't expect it to happen so quickly. I'm totally amazed."

She's now written more than a hundred books, including nonfiction, children's books, women's fiction and myriad books for teens. It's the books for teen readers, however, that capture her heart. Her work includes numerous books in the Diary of a Teenage Girl series, the Color Me series with nine books, the Degrees of Guilt series, as well as the book *Piercing Proverbs: Wise Words for Today's Teens* and By Design Bible study series for teen girls. According to Carlson, it's a market that is often misunderstood.

First, teen novels are not easy to write.

"It's tough to write teen novels because teens are really good at sniffing out what is authentic and what isn't. Some writers think that because their adult novels aren't selling they should write for teens," Carlson says. "If you're not cutting it in the adult market, don't assume that you're going to cut it in the teen market."

Also, teens aren't about to be preached at.

"I've heard people say, 'You can really preach at them through your books because it's such an important time in their lives.' But you have to be more clever than that," says Carlson.

Big Changes   When Carlson's novel *Diary of a Teenage Girl* came out in 2000, her publisher was both worried and careful. Worried because editors weren't sure how the market would react to subjects such as drugs, alcohol, sex, cutting, and anorexia. Careful because they didn't want to drive readers away.

"Five years ago, the Christian market and publishers were saying 'We don't know if we can say that, we don't know if we can do that,'" says Carlson. "There was a fear of having the book hit the market and some little bookstore lady say, 'Oh, the girl gets pregnant in this book!'"

Even more recently Carlson and the publisher of another of her teen series had discussions on how many times she could use the word "crap" in her books. For the first book, no "crap." For the second, two "crap"s and two "freakings."

"Now, a year later, they say 'Don't worry about it; just do what you want because we trust you,'" Carlson says with a laugh.

Five years after those first discussions, Carlson feels she and other writers can be more forthright in language, situation, and content. Teens, after all, are exposed to these issues and activities and want to understand how to handle them.

"I've toned some things down, but at least we've pushed the envelope, not to be shocking but to reach these girls," says Carlson.

The response has been overwhelmingly positive.

"About 99.9 percent of what I hear from teen readers is 'Thank you, thank you, I can never talk to my parents about this,'" says Carlson. "So in a way I'm doing what I said I shouldn't: I'm preaching at the kids, but they just don't know it."

Breaking into   This experienced writer for teens offers good
the Market   advice for writers eager to break into the teen
                     market.

First, hone your writing skills. "Don't assume it's a lesser market," she says.

Second, immerse yourself in teen culture, teen language, and teen problems.

Carlson remembers vividly her sons' teenage years, she taps her nieces for information on language and conflicts, and she reads teen magazines and books.

"I actually force myself to watch MTV sometimes," she says.

She also shamelessly eavesdrops on teen conversations wherever she is.

Finally, avoid being what she calls "too stylish."

"It's a tightrope walk to have the book be real and talk the way teens talk without being out of date too soon," she says. "You want to sound timely, but you don't want to sound goofy."

Writers also need to understand that teen readers, especially girls, are immersed in the internal stuff of life: relationships, inner struggles, friendships.

These issues haven't changed much since Carlson was a teenager and probably won't change in the future, either.

"Kids are always going to be here," she says. "The intensity of issues has changed. While it's still boyfriends, best friends, and parents, we now talk about divorce, someone getting pregnant, petting, or anorexia."

Writing Regimen Carlson calls herself a "fast writer," writing a chapter or more a day. Each morning she briefly goes over her work from the day before to get herself back into the story, then heads right into the next portion of the book.

"It gets me into the character's head and connected with the story. That way I don't get in a quagmire. In my early writing days I often threw away the first chapter. But now if I sat there and obsessed over it I would never get to the end of the book. I just keep going and get that first draft done," says Carlson. She figures she gets five to six good hours of writing in a day.

"You'll never be able to really edit yourself until the whole book is done anyway; anything you do before the book is done is just tweaking."

Carlson doesn't outline her books, though she concedes that many writers do.

"I like to be surprised and I always am," she says. "I think if I'm being surprised there's a greater chance my readers will be, too. To me it's just fun."

Despite writing many books in numerous series for young adults, Carlson is still a one-book writer. She writes one at a time, sticking with it until the manuscript is done.

"When the writer part of me kicks in, I throw organization out the window. That's why it's really good for me to do one book at a time. But whether it's a children's book, a teen book, or an adult novel, the elements are the same. You need a strong character and you need to care about your characters. Your character needs problems. Depending on the age group, the problems get bigger and more complicated. I really believe that story is key no matter the age group."

 About Melody Carlson:

Did you know . . .

She wrote her first short story long hand, her first young adult novel on a typewriter.

Her first book was *How to Start a Quality Childcare Business in Your Home: Everything You Need to Know.*

She once led the children's department at Multnomah Publishers. Her first children's books and several teen novels were published by Multnomah, and ten years later she now authors a popular teen series published by them.

She writes about ten books a year and works with numerous publishers.

She's written a screenplay and dreams of making the leap to film.

For more information on Melody Carlson, visit her website at www.melodycarlson.com.

Chapter 18

Nancy Rue 'TWEEN THE LINES
Nancy Rue

*"I think that the Christian market for tweens
is much more open, but I also have a clear
understanding of what things are never going to be okay.
We can't use any kind of swear word,
no obscene language and I'm fine with that.
I want readers to trust me."*

Nancy Rue knows the heart of tweens, those confusing, exhil-arating eight- to twelve-year-olds. She knows their struggles, joys, needs, and desires. Best, though, she knows how to write what they want to read.

Rue has learned much through her sixteen years as a teacher, her speaking ministry, and raising her daughter. She has written about eighty books, some for teen readers and adults, but most for tweens. The Lily Series (Zonderkidz) includes fourteen fiction and twelve nonfiction titles. She also authored thirty books in the Christian Heritage series published by Focus on the Family. She is currently immersed in Zonderkidz' FaithGirlz! line that includes the Sophie series for tween girls. Sophie is in sixth grade in books 1-6, and seventh grade in books 7-12. Rue is also contributing to the FaithGirlz! Bible.

Meet the Tweens   Eight to twelve-year-olds are voracious read-ers and big consumers, though most books are purchased by others. "Books are one of the main things tweens ask for from adults," says Rue.

Tweens are passionate about where they are in life. Their inter-ests are blossoming, their personalities are coming into focus, and friends are incredibly important. Girls and boys this age also watch closely and learn from those around them.

"It's a very important time spiritually, because they are so much more open to things like grace and miracles and the whole mystery of salvation. It's a pretty standard statistic that 80 percent of Christians make their commitment to Christ before the age of twelve," Rue says.

Tweens also love to have a character they can get to know and follow; they love to collect all books in a series. Rue has met girls who won't buy the current book in her series because they haven't read the previous books yet.

They also like to know what the rules are. Following the rules is sometimes another story, but they at least like to know what the rules are.

"Their little minds are more linear, and they like order despite the chaos in their rooms," Rue says with a laugh. "They like to know what to expect."

Writing for Tweens Tween novels are compact, with only about 120 pages in each book. That's about 30,000 words, or twelve chapters of ten pages each, to tell the story.

"If you go over that, you are going to have to cut it," says Rue.

Rue writes with her series in mind, first developing her main character then deciding the series's hook. Finally she chooses the setting for the series.

On character: "To me it's all about character. What are her challenges? What are her qualities and how do they sometimes serve her well and sometimes not? How did she get that way? What's her family situation and what challenges does that create for her? What kind of people aren't going to like her?"

On hook: "What do I want for Lily or for Sophie by the end of the series, and what is the best way to get there? What is going to tie the books together? With Lily it was that she is always looking for her niche in life because her family all seem to have theirs."

On place: Rue's settings are usually real places. Sophie, for instance, lives in Virginia, while Lily lives in Burlington, New Jersey. Place determines activities her characters engage in, clothing choices, vacation spots, even food.

Rue lives every character. For the Sophie series, she has Sophie keep a diary; so Rue writes that diary first, which often leads to interesting plot twists. When the Lily series ended, Rue mourned.

"I missed her. I missed knowing that she was there. I didn't think anyone could be as wonderful as Lily. But now I love Sophie and I'm relieved that girls love her too," says Rue.

Honesty is a big key to writing effectively for tween readers. These kids know fake, they know when they're being talked down to.

"I have always had to be honest about what I'm seeing and then ask myself 'How do girls navigate that?'" says Rue. "One of the things I really emphasize is the importance of having a good circle of friends who know how to treat each other and are not horrible to each other."

Writing Process   Rue begins each writing day by spending an hour-and-a-half to two hours meeting God. She journals, reads the Bible, uses commentaries, and prays—whatever it takes to get centered on God.

"I feel like I have a huge obligation to get my spiritual life right for the girls," says Rue.

After a quick walk, she is usually at her desk by 8 a.m. dealing first with office details and then writing from 9 a.m. until midafternoon. She often eats lunch at her desk.

Research is a big part of any book Rue writes. She records information on 3x5 cards, uses colored file folders, and creates a timeline for each book. She uses a binder to organize information she gathers, from pictures of haircuts and bedroom decor to geographical information for the setting. She includes sections for the theme, plot, characters, setting, and other details such as Sophie's school schedule to make sure she gets the daily timeline right.

"I know that if I just sat down and started writing I'd be a nervous wreck. I need to know where I'm going with a book and how I'm going to get there," Rue says.

When working on multiple projects, such as the Sophie series and her 'Nama Beach High series for teens, she simply puts away the binder for that book and opens another.

Wide Open Market   Five years ago Rue would have talked about restrictions and limitations put on Christian novels for tweens. Now, she says, those restrictions are gone. That doesn't mean there aren't a few rules.

"I think that the Christian market for tweens is much more open, but I also have a clear understanding of what things are never going to be okay. We can't use any kind of swear word, no obscene language, and I'm fine with that. I want readers to trust me," says Rue.

The tween market will only become more important, according to Rue, because people are becoming more aware of the importance of this age group.

"I think the community is waking up to the fact that the Christian formation at this age is incredible and we need to be paying attention," she says.

"Authors must keep writing good books for this age because there are so many things vying for kids' attention—video games, television, DVDs, iPods. We need to be careful not to think that the kids won't notice if our writing is bad or not authentic."

Read about Nancy Rue, Lily, and Sophie at www.nancyrue.com.

Chapter 19

A Well Heeled Approach to Children's Books

Damon Taylor

"If a book makes two different points,
which one will the kids take?
Normally neither because they're confused.
I drive that one point, but not enough to annoy parents
so that they're looking for a sharp object
when the kids ask for the book again and again."

Damon Taylor took what he calls a "backdoor approach" to writing for children. Now his 16-book Child Sockology series and his new God Can Use Me series (Kregel Publications) are flying out the *front* doors of bookstores across the country.

Taylor started out as an illustrator. He presented his artwork to several publishers, then mentioned the children's series he was working on. Kregel loved both his illustrations and his book ideas, agreeing to publish the series.

The first Child Sockology books, four story and four board books, were released in 2001. There are now eight of each. The more recent God Can Use Me series for kids features animals used uniquely by God despite their weaknesses and fears.

Taylor's goal is to create books that entertain and teach children while appealing to the adults who must read them aloud. He's learned several lessons along the way.

The key to writing children's books is one clear, simple message, offers Taylor, who narrows the focus of his main point to avoid the confusion that comes with competing messages.

"If a book makes two different points, which one will the kids take? Normally neither because they're confused," says Taylor. "I drive that one point, but not enough to annoy parents so they're looking for a sharp object when the kids ask for the book again and again."

He asks himself, "What are the kids going to get?" then builds *into* that, not onto it. He retells the biblical story in a unique way, offering young readers the further step of application.

"Even Jesus used stories and parables to make his point," says Taylor.

Illustrations are central to Taylor's work. He uses bright colors and simple backgrounds, making the main character the focal point of each cartoon-like page.

"I don't want to give kids a Thomas Kinkaid kind of painting because they're too young for that," says Taylor whose books are geared toward children ages four and up. "Most kids that age respond to cartoons much more than they do to serious illustrations done in watercolor or whatever."

Simple illustrations don't mean stupid, however. Taylor throws something into the background that could prompt questions from a child. In one illustration it's a millstone used to grind wheat. In another it's sheep.

"The main character is always the focal point, but background things can get adults involved in answering questions," says Taylor.

He's also not above throwing in the odd "Zoinks!" for Scooby Doo fans, and jokes about Eli's Cheesecake for Chicagoland dwellers.

"With children it's simple and it's funny. They look at a page and say, 'Oh look, he's got a big nose' and they laugh. I think if you're going to get a point across it's easier to do with humor," Taylor says. "Also, you have to make the point quickly."

But how does a children's writer tell the stories of Esther and Joseph, for example, without talking about sensitive issues that kids don't understand? Taylor realizes kids won't (and don't need to) understand the nuances of Esther's relationship with the king, but they do understand that Esther was a beautiful woman, she was afraid, and that she overcame her fear to save her people. The message of facing fear and following God is plenty clear without the added layers. He also relies heavily on his editing team at Kregel to make sure he isn't changing the gist of the biblical story.

Taylor offers this advice for aspiring children's book authors:
1. "Don't ever take it personally if someone says no to you. God gives people visions at certain times and you can't expect everyone to pick up on yours," he says. "You've got to be thick-skinned about

others' reactions to your work. Maybe they have some insight to give you that will clear your vision, allow you to grow."

2. Taylor knows his success is from God. As the tongue-tied son of a minister, he never thought he'd find a way for God to use him to share the message of Christ.

"Now I'm enjoying the way God is using me. It's fun to be able to share Christ with children through my writing and illustrating. I think God puts things in my heart to do, then leaves it there and kind of pokes me, saying 'Remember?'"

3. Taylor encourages writers to avoid going into children's books for the money.

"Don't ever expect to make a dime," he laughs. "If money is the goal, there are many other easier ways to make money than to write or illustrate children's books. But I feel God is leading me and directing me to write these books."

He hasn't given up his day job, however.

"Supporting my family would be great, but I'm not going to sit around expecting it. God's not saying 'I'm going to give you this idea and it's going to make you rich.' It's more like, 'I'm going to give you this idea and you have to get it done.'"

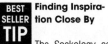 **Finding Inspiration Close By**

The Sockology series began in the bedroom of Taylor's son Coleman. Taylor and his wife Bridget heard then-3-year-old Coleman hollering "Oh, oh, help help!" They rushed upstairs to find Coleman sitting on the bed surrounded by every sock in the house. He was smashing them together, throwing them around, creating characters that talked and yelled.

"Sometimes we would notice that he was a little intense, maybe having a bad day. He had a baby sister he didn't ask for, and he was kind of working out his stress and his problems by playing with his socks," recalls Taylor. "He would be mad at his sister and would say things like, 'Shelby, ahhh, throw her over the edge.'"

Taylor wrote his first book based on Coleman's sock escapades. *Commander Cole and the Sock Patrol* was never published; however, it became the basis for the Child Sockology series.

"It's about a little boy who plays with his socks and remembers Bible stories with help from his buddy Sock-ariah, and from that works out his problems by applying biblical truths," says Taylor.

His books still feature Coleman and Shelby, who are now teenagers.

Chapter 20

BOARD BOOK BONANZA
Crystal Bowman

*"What makes a board book challenging is word count.
Every word is there for a reason."*

Crystal Bowman wrote her first poem at age ten, never thinking that it might be difficult to write in perfect rhythm and rhyme. Her teacher was blown away, she says, telling Bowman she'd end up a poet. Since then she's written many poems for children and for special occasions, numerous song lyrics, and several published books.

She also turns her wordsmithing to writing board books—those short, little books with pages tough enough for young children to gnaw on. Her latest batch (for Zonderkidz) is slated for release from Fall 2005 through Spring 2007.

"Board books are not for children learning to read; they are for children learning to talk," says Bowman. "They are designed so that an adult reads to the child."

Board books may seem easy to write, but Bowman knows otherwise. Each one tests her ability to find the right words, to convey a spiritual truth, to write at appropriate age level, and to keep both child and adult interested.

Characteristics of good board books include:

1. Limited word count. Board books for babies have one or two words per page; board books for toddlers can have as many as 300 total, with an average of twenty-five words per page. They typically run twelve to twenty-four pages, with one idea per 2-page spread. Because of such limited word count, every noun and verb must be strong.

"What makes a board book challenging is word count," Bowman says. "Every word is there for a reason."

Occasionally board books are designed with no words to allow for creativity in storytelling on the part of the reader.

2. Well planned illustrations. Children need simple illustrations of concrete objects that coincide with accompanying text. The art must also be age-appropriate. Though most writers don't create their own art, it behooves writers to make sure text and art match.

Bowman's contract stipulates that she must see her words on the page with the art to make sure, for example, that the black horse she wrote about is not a gray horse in the picture.

"I am willing to change my text just so it doesn't look stupid," she says. "Every author I talk to has a horror story about this."

While art for the youngest children must be simple, art in books for older children can be a little more elaborate. It can not only enhance the story, but go a step further than the words.

Bowman says the bottom line is, "If you can't visualize it, it doesn't belong in a board book. Kids are just learning words, which is why pictures have to be so concrete in a board book."

3. Age-appropriate content. Often board books are designed to help children learn shapes, colors, numbers and the alphabet. Others, however, can teach simple biblical principles such as obedience, being sorry, and God's love.

"It's critical that the biblical issues or spiritual truths be presented in a positive way that children can comprehend," says Bowman. "It's also important for parents to remember that children can enjoy a book written below their age level. It's enjoyable and relaxing for them."

4. Well done rhythm and rhyme. Though many board books are not written in rhyme, those that are must flow evenly and smoothly and use natural language. So natural, says Bowman, that readers are hardly aware of how the words fit together. In fact, the rhyming words should almost be predictable.

"When rhythm is awkward and rhymes are forced, it makes reading an unpleasant and annoying experience," she says.

Writing in rhyme adds another challenge to a book already restricted by word count, vocabulary, and concept.

"It's better to go without rhythm and rhyme than to do it badly," says Bowman. "But it's very age appropriate. Young children are born with a sense of rhythm. They respond to music, clapping, and tapping."

Bowman has written some board books in just a day, while others have taken her weeks. She likes to search out the best word or phrase, constantly tweaking as she goes.

"The key for me in making a quality board book is to write it, then leave it alone for a day or two. If something's wrong it will jump off the page," she says. "If you can write an enjoyable, playful, and positive story using 200 words or less, age appropriate language, and natural and precise rhythm and rhyme, you can write a quality board book."

Crystal Bowman is a member of American Christian Writers (www. ACWriters.com) and Society of Children's Book Writers and Illustrators (www.scbwi.org).

Jerry Jenkins
Terri Blackstock Lauren Winner
Karen Kingsbury
James Scott Bell Brandilyn Collins Angela Elwell Hunt Davis Bunn
Melody Carlson
Charlene Ann Baumbich
Sally Stuart
Jack Cavanaugh Nancy Rue
Barbara Nicolosi Justin Lookadoo
Dennis Hensley Dave Lambert & Lin Johnson

SECTION FIVE

Master the Specifics: Learning from Genre Experts

Chapter 21

THE RISKY BUSINESS OF SUSPENSE

Brandilyn Collins

"We live in a very evil world and that's reality; ...
Why not give Christians an alternative?
Give them a good, strong suspense novel
that has God's message woven into it."

Moving into the suspense genre wasn't without risk for Brandilyn Collins. Her women's fiction was well received, but she needed to stick with one genre. Suspense, however, is relatively new on the Christian fiction scene and its appearance energized fans and critics alike.

Collins has received some e-mails suggesting that Christian books shouldn't include violence, that she's flirting with the devil in some of her books.

"The question 'How can you write that and still be a Christian?' is very interesting and one that needs to be addressed," she says. "Suspense is quite new in Christian fiction. In the past five years it's really exploded."

The lure, she says, is that suspense fiction is realistic. Its power manifests itself in sheer numbers of movies and television shows that have to do with crime or suspense, a trend Collins sees as beneficial to her kind of writing.

"We live in a very evil world and that's reality; more and more people want fiction to represent that reality. There are a lot of people out there who love suspense, and in the general market it has been very successful. Why not give Christians an alternative? Give them a good, strong suspense novel that has God's message woven into it," says Collins.

Her work is deliciously scary, full of villains and good people trying to catch them. She gets many of her ideas from true crime television shows and reading the newspaper. The premise isn't the hard part, she says. The hard part is coming up with the entire plot.

"My suspense is known for high twists and surprises. It's fast-paced, but it's hard to come up with that intensity book after book," she says.

Collins is a self-taught fiction writer. When she decided to pursue a fiction writing career, she began the long process of learning the craft. She likes to say she put herself through her own college.

That college was 50 percent reading and 50 percent writing. She read novels galore, and she read books on how to write fiction.

"I would read novels with pen in hand and mark them up. I'd think about what struck me about point-of-view and foreshadowing. I learned to read into the symbolism, about characterization. I also learned what not to do," she says.

She attended one weekend workshop that helped her immensely, but relied heavily on how-to books and her background in drama.

"I studied and studied and studied. I tell people who are learning to write fiction that it takes years. I know you hear about people who write their first book and sell it. Those stories become news because they're unusual, not the norm," says Collins.

She likens learning to build a story to learning to build a house. The architect must go through college to learn his trade, builders must learn their trades as well. The idea for a story, or dreaming about a house, is a very small portion of the project. And learning the right skills is neither optional nor easy.

Just as Collins taught herself to write, she also teaches others. She usually teaches fiction writing at three writers conferences each year. Over the years she's targeted several key areas where beginning writers need the most help:

1. Complex character emotion. New authors, and even newly published authors, struggle with character emotions that are too shallow or too one-at-a-time.

"Human emotion does not work that way. Emotions are intertwined, with one emotion jumping off another, and very complex. Writers need to keep that in mind."

2. Rhythm. The beat of sentences must match the beat of emotion that the author wants readers to feel.

"Sentences have to vary, but it depends on what I want to do. If

I'm in a high action scene, sentences will shorten. They might be phrases or one word. You do that purposely until it gets tedious and you have to switch lengths. It's something I continue to learn."

3. Story structure. Structure involves pace and tone and plotting. It comes, she says, from reading and learning.

4. Understanding that writing isn't easy. "I drive myself crazy. Writing is so hard. I wish it came as easily as teaching writing. I'm on my knees with every book saying, 'Oh God, please help me finish this book because I don't know what I'm doing. I'm a terrible writer, I'll never get this done, I'm up against a wall.'"

She'd never give up her job writing Christian suspense, despite the critics and, occasionally, even her own horror at what she produces.

"Sometimes I write something, like the prologue for the fourth book in the Hidden Faces series, *Web of Lies*, and I totally creep myself out," she says with a laugh. "I used to be such a sweet, nice person. My poor mother doesn't know what to make of me."

Collins discusses how she writes Christian suspense on her web log entitled "Forensics and Faith" (www.forensicsandfaith.blogspot. com). Part of the discussion is reproduced here, used with her permission.

From www.forensicsandfaith.blogspot.com:

Every day when I sit down to write, I pray the same beleaguered prayer—"Oh, please, God, don't let me be boring!" I find it plain difficult to keep my stories moving at the pace my readers have come to expect. So what have I done in the Hidden Faces books when my protagonist, Annie, is working on a forensic art project? I mean, how exciting is watching somebody draw, or sculpt, or whatever? Here are a few answers I've come up with:

1. Inject tension into the scene. This tension spills from all the trouble in which Annie currently finds herself. Her concentration will shift from what she's doing to the fears she's facing of what's to come. I don't want to give away any story lines, so I'll talk about this generally. In *Brink of Death*, Annie must interview Erin after she (Erin) witnesses her mother's murder. The girl is still half in shock

Drama in Writing

Brandilyn Collins also has a background in drama. She majored in drama in college (before switching to journalism) and has seen some of the techniques she learned translate into her writing. One key area is characterization. Each of her characters is unique, and each one carries complex emotions, something inherent in method acting. Collins also uses her understanding of whole emotion memory to write about characters who are very different from herself.

"Basically, every human being has experienced every emotion out there. It's a matter of taking those emotions to the max when you've got to write about, say, a serial killer," she says.

The techniques Collins used in method acting were so much a part of her writing that it surprised her when other writers had no idea what she was talking about.

"These techniques were so fundamental to the way I wrote that I ended up writing a book in which I took secrets from method acting and adapted them to use in writing a novel."

"Getting Into Character: Seven Secrets a Novelist Can Learn From Actors" was released in 2002 by John Wiley & Sons.

and petrified of seeing "The Face" of the killer again—even on paper. Annie is petrified that she'll mess up the assignment (in this book, forensic art is new to her). These books are in first person from Annie's point of view. But I use lots of perception on her part of what Erin is thinking/feeling, based on Erin's actions, expressions, and tone of voice. And I inject Annie's fears of the future—What if I get this drawing wrong, what if I skew Erin's memory? We could be looking for the wrong man while the real killer roams among us … .

2. Draw out the tension until it reaches a breaking point, then end the chapter. This is the ol' "hook" that we writers talk about. In *Brink of Death*, for example, I tried to make the tension build and build to the moment when the drawing's finally done, and Erin must lower her eyes to look at it. By this time, she's shaking and so is Annie. Everything has built to this moment. Everything else that happens in the story depends on Erin's reaction to what Annie has drawn. So she lowers her eyes … Boom. End chapter.

3. Don't let that taut line go now! Egads, the next chapter has to keep the tension just as much. So I don't want to answer the hook's "what happens?" question in the first paragraph. Instead I introduce another problem—one Annie and Erin must work on together. Here we go again—build tension, build it, build it. Until the whole sequence finally ends with a major event—of course, at the end of a chapter.

However, I have to remember that tension is only one thread of this entire sequence. The other thread is what's actually happening—the interview questions, Annie drawing—all the things a forensic artist must do, the materials she must use. The trick for me is to interweave these two threads into a complex tapestry of emotion and action. The forensic art process is fascinating in itself—to a point. However it could become boring very quickly if I spend too many paragraphs on that thread without a break.

http://forensicsandfaith.blogspot.com/2005_02_01_
forensicsandfaith_archive.html

Chapter 22

Julie Ann Barnhill

FINDING THE
HOT-BUTTON ISSUES
Julie Ann Barnhill

*"I think it's equal parts personal inspiration
and divine inspiration,
but it's also doing your homework
as far as knowing and talking to people."*

M ost people say you need a platform to sell your books. I say you need a platform to find your books," says Julie Ann Barnhill.

Barnhill's first book, *She's Gonna Blow! Real Help for Moms Dealing with Anger* (Harvest House, 2001) has sold more than 100,000 copies. The idea for the book, she says, came from her own life and her fledgling speaking career. She spoke at MOPS (Mothers of Preschoolers) groups and women's groups, eventually speaking at Hearts at Home conferences. Her workshop on moms and anger drew large audiences and positive response.

It was that response that got her thinking seriously about a book. When she met up with several Harvest House editors, she spoke of her book idea. Later she wrote a proposal, which Harvest House accepted. *She's Gonna Blow!* was published in 2001, with an updated version released in 2005.

She's been a featured guest on *Oprah, Focus on the Family,* and a host of other programs, as well as written more books: *Til Debt Do Us Part* (Harvest House, 2002), *Scandalous Grace* (2004), *Radical Forgiveness* (2005), and *Exquisite Hope* (2005) (all published by Tyndale) and *Motherhood: The Guilt that Keeps on Giving* (Harvest House, 2006).

Barnhill wasn't surprised at the success of *She's Gonna Blow!*

"In my workshops and presentations I came face to face with moms. I knew moms were desperate for somebody who would talk about this topic, who would say, 'This is where I've been, it's probably where you are, and there's hope,'" she says.

While there's no scientific method to predicting those hot issues that yield hot books, Barnhill offers several suggestions.

First, she listens to herself. The issues she struggles with, such as anger and finances and guilt, become the basis for books.

"*She's Gonna Blow*! came solely out of my desire to read a book like it," she says. "I would look in bookstores and ask, 'Do you have anything for women who wish they'd never had kids?' They'd look at me like there was something wrong with me, and that's where the book was born."

Second, she listens to those around her. The women she spoke to and talk with faced the same things she did. She heard women talk about finances and guilt, forgiveness and grace.

"You think there's a need and you speak on it; you can pick up after just a few seconds whether that need is just your problem or there really is something *deeper*," Barnhill says. "I think it's equal parts personal inspiration and divine inspiration, but it's also doing your homework as far as knowing and talking to people."

Her book *Scandalous Grace* came out of speaking engagements and just listening. "It speaks of the marvelous grace of God, who loves us women despite our frailties," she explains.

"I think you have to be sensitive to what people are talking about around you. Then you dig a little deeper to what people are really saying," says Barnhill.

Third, she works on seeing the big picture. The key to a hot-button book is being ahead of the culture curve and appealing to a vast audience of people, Christian or not, who are struggling with common issues such as body image, anger, happiness, or debt.

"I never want to cower from our culture. I want to jump right in the middle of it. I think truth brings freedom," says Barnhill.

Fourth, she narrows the target for her book. Sure, a speaking platform is a great thing for selling books. It's also a great way to narrow the focus for book ideas.

"Speaking tempers me so I don't just get this wild-hair idea and go off and think everybody wants it. I find out very quickly how to balance that idea and whether or not I'm on target with that topic," says Barnhill.

Fifth, and most importantly, Barnhill hands the book and the success over to God. The bottom line, she says, is that God wanted her to have a bestseller to get into the heads and hearts of men and women who needed to hear the message.

"Clearly the success, the Oprah and Dr. Dobson interviews and all that, is what God wanted. Only God could do those things," she says.

Marketing Plays a Huge Role There's no getting around it: Barnhill loves to market her books. She's mystified by authors who don't like to talk about their work when all she does is talk about hers. She's got several strategies for getting the word out.

The first strategy is to go right to the top, go right to the biggest market, talk to the most powerful people.

"What have you got to lose? They can just say no," Barnhill says with a laugh. "It's like we're apologizing for being enthusiastic about our ideas and dreams God has given us."

Second, have materials that "scream who you are." Barnhill created marketing materials that are distinctive, that catch people's eyes. Brochures, letters, and her website reflect her personality and her message.

"Your personality has to come out in your books and your materials. It's hand and glove," she says.

Third, she talks to the people who know the business and listens to what they say.

"I have big ideas and dreams, but, boy, do I know when to shut up and listen to someone who knows what they're talking about," says Barnhill.

The bottom line? "Being who you are and reveling in it because we're one of a kind and here for a short time," says Barnhill.

How to Hit the Hot Buttons

1. Listen to yourself.

2. Listen to those around you.

3. Look at the big cultural picture.

4. Narrow the focus of the book.

5. Let God be in charge.

For more information on Julie Barnhill, her speaking and her writing, visit www.juliebarnhill.com.

Chapter 23

Sex Jumpstarts a New Conversation
Lauren Winner

*"I think we need to strip away euphemism and tell the truth,
and this is not necessarily translated into who
can be the most explicit about body parts.
The mere fact that the evangelical community is saying
'Let's take seriously the fact that we're created
with bodies' is a step forward."*

Lauren Winner's most recent book, *Real Sex*, shouldn't have shocked too many people. After all, she wrote her memoir, *Girl Meets God*, at age twenty-four; so her having the audacity to write on sex and chastity wasn't a surprise. The topic wasn't the problem. What stretched her, she says, was finding the idiom in which to write about her own sexual sins. And if Winner has trouble writing about sex, imagine the struggles facing the church.

The plethora of Christian sex books available today is a sign that Christians are willing to address the issue. Winner, however, suggests we go one step further.

"I think we need to strip away euphemism and tell the truth, and this is not necessarily translated into who can be the most explicit about body parts," she says. "The mere fact that the evangelical community is saying 'Let's take seriously the fact that we're created with bodies' is a step forward."

Explicit means addressing the truth that sex usually feels good even if it happens outside of marriage, and we don't automatically feel guilty about it, either. It means understanding that chastity is a spiritual discipline, not just another "don't" for single Christians. It means acknowledging that the heavy-handed "no" we hear about premarital sex from childhood on doesn't immediately become an unencumbered "yes" the moment marriage vows are spoken. Traditional Christianity has done a good job of relegating the body (and by extension sex) to a list of dos and don'ts. The body is just a tool, a necessary evil, in building true spirituality.

"For women in particular, we get mixed messages about our bodies and what it means to be a good girl. We know we feel bodily desire, but we're not necessarily hearing in the Christian community that that is how we're made," she says. "I think when women find a Christian resource that expounds that, there is a sense of relief to learn 'I'm not crazy or sinful.'"

Telling the Truth   Winner's call for more explicitness in conversations about sex is not about body parts but instead about how God created us and how our bodies are part of who we are as humans and God-followers. God created sex to stay within marriage, but the question is why? Was it merely a legalistic statement about context, or does God have something for us to learn from sex both inside and outside marriage?

"It seems to me that married sex is quite different from unmarried sex," she says. "I think the church can do better when it comes to articulating why it is good news that sex belongs in marriage. What should married sex look like?

"We need to talk about it because there's no neutral way to live in our bodies, and we're going to get messages about sex from somewhere," she says. The discussion isn't about sex, but about how we view our bodies created by God. After all, "sex is not the most important thing on the planet."

Sex and the   "In writing about sex and Christianity explicitly, I
Spiritual Life   can't keep it separated from what's going on in my spiritual life. I could say 'Now I'm going to write about sexual sin,' but it sparked further self-scrutiny and repentance on my part as I was working on the book," admits Winner. "It wasn't merely a writing project."

Another struggle she faced was articulating what she knew intuitively to be true about chastity and sex in the Christian context. For example, she was certain that sex, more than an individual act, is a communal event.

"But articulating what that looks like and *why* in nonintuitive terms is much more difficult," says Winner.

She regularly visits Christian colleges and churches to talk to students about sexuality, among other things. She leaves with a strong sense that there need to be "resources that are less pomp and more honest and in touch with the culture we actually live in."

One interesting phenomenon that occurred with the release of *Real Sex* is the interest it generated in the secular media, from newspaper articles to reviews to radio interviews.

"Maybe society has gotten so crazy and the sexual revolution has gone to such an extreme that even the most secular person can diagnose that we don't want our 13-year-olds having oral sex," she says. "Maybe that is a place where Christians and non-Christians can come together and have a conversation where we don't see each other as antagonists."

Winner's goal was not to generate controversy within the church, though controversy is probably a sure thing, considering the topic.

"If absolutely every evangelical in the country loved *Real Sex*, I would have done something wrong," she says. "I did not want to write the same book about chastity we've already read eighteen times. My goal was not to convert the secular world to Christian chastity; my goal was to reconfigure a particular conversation in the Church."

For more information on *Real Sex*, visit www.brazospress.com.
To learn more about Lauren Winner, visit www.laurenwinner.net.

Chapter 24

Justin Lookadoo

THE DIRT ON
WRITING ABOUT SEX
Justin Lookadoo

*"I'm all about having a strong spiritual life,
but 'just pray about it' does not work.
You better give readers something they can do,
something to help them handle the situation."*

T he *Dirt on Sex* isn't for older adults. In fact, most adults would
be horrified at what Justin Lookadoo writes on subjects many
consider to be private. Conservative Christians lambast him
for being too honest, liberals for including God in his message.

Whatever. Justin's going to write what adolescents and young
adults need and want to hear in a language and style they understand. Sure, his publisher (Revell) may take a few hits from conservative types. But it is willing to go out on a limb in the interest of
truth. Lookadoo's books are all about honesty. Naked truth. Tough
truth. Hilarious, naked, tough truth.

"I've been labeled the speaker and writer for the ADD generation. I make the book fun, make it like a magazine," he says, "because words on a piece of paper are a textbook, and why would
somebody want to read a textbook outside of class?"

Lookadoo writes how he speaks, which means he's holding a
conversation with his readers about subjects that may be embar-
rassing but are certainly important.

"Kids are looking for somebody to be involved with them, to actually care about where they're at and understand where they're at,"
he says. "In a question-and-answer book, adults make up the questions and write the answers, but they aren't including the questions
most teenagers want to ask. Most questions they have, they can't
verbalize."

Writing a book on a touchy subject such as sex carries a host
of difficulties. The major one, says Lookadoo, is finding out what

truth is. Ultraconservatives and ultraliberals are so adept at spinning facts to meet their agendas that truth is hard to come by. What, for example, are the real statistics on condom use? What are the real stats on the number of teens having sex? How much do Christian teens know, and what are they doing with each other?

"When I say truth I'm talking about factual truth, not ultimate Truth. Connecting to Scripture is easy. Lots of books lose the teen audience because they connect to Scripture, but that's it. If you're a teen struggling with your girlfriend about sexual behavior, you can quote Romans all day long, but what you need are practical ways to get out of the situation," says Lookadoo. "I'm all about having a strong spiritual life, but 'just pray about it' does not work. You better give readers something they can do, something to help them handle the situation."

Many authors find it difficult to move from biblical teaching to real-world application. Not Lookadoo. He does 350 programs a year in middle and high schools, and he knows what teens are thinking and going through and doing on Saturday night. It's what he calls his own "fast track to reality."

The easy part of writing such a book is finding the passion to do it.

"You've got to have the passion if you're going to connect with the audience. Finding the passion is easy for me because I see every day the destruction that sex is causing," he says.

His modus operandi for writing books on traditionally difficult subjects is to first get everything down, as harshly and honestly as possible. He writes longhand on yellow tablets. He then tones down his original work in deference to his Christian publisher and his mom.

"I ask 'What are the words my mom says I can't say in public anymore?' and I remove those words," he says. Almost hard to believe, considering the words that appear in *The Dirt on Sex.*

He then looks for stories to augment his points, calling on his counseling experience and conversations with teens and adults. He then puts what he calls his own spin on the manuscript.

"It's hugely important to be personal because, if you're talking about intimate issues, it needs to be a conversation. I need to get into their lives," says Lookadoo.

He does that first through creating connection, then through getting their attention. These steps allow him to talk about the real issues related to sex.

"When kids read the book they hear it being loud, obnoxious, and sarcastic, which relates to every teen guy and that also relates to every teen girl who knows a teen guy, so we have a connection. Then I give them a warning that if they're easily offended they should walk away. That gets their attention," says Lookadoo.

While his writing is in-your-face, funny, and pretty darn graphic, it's a well planned, even calculated, approach. Lookadoo lives and breathes teens. He hangs out with them, sees their movies, listens to their music, and reads their magazines. He also hangs out with college students because that's who high school and junior high kids want to be.

"Is it calculated in the fact that I sit down and write A, B, and C? No. Is it calculated in that I purposefully put myself in the lifestyle and environment? Yes."

Yes, he's taken some heat for *The Dirt on Sex* and his other books. He's also had to work with his publisher to keep his writing style intact, incomplete sentences and all. They've come to an understanding that works for both.

Lookadoo's books are popular, no doubt about it. He and Revell are planning other projects, and Justin's speaking ministry is growing. He faces censure, however, from public schools who don't want him to talk about God, and churches whose "perception of total honesty is not their teenagers' perception of total honesty."

Sometimes he tones down his message, depending on where he is and if he wants to be invited back, and other times he shoots with both barrels. He continues to be surprised by teens' questions about issues of sexuality, but not surprised at the sexual activity of teens, Christian and not.

BEST SELLER TIP: A Look at Justin Lookadoo

Justin Lookadoo is a Southern gentleman born and bred.

OK, maybe not gentleman in the polite, well dressed, shaking hands kind of way.

He's a wild Texan with weird hair who talks a lot. But that doesn't stop him from being the kind of man who tells it like it is and who loves teenagers enough to be honest with them.

He's been a juvenile probation officer; a consultant for educational, corporate, and safety concerns; and a sought-after speaker for conferences, schools, and churches.

Along with all that, he's written some pretty cool books: *Datable: Are You? Are They?* with Hayley DeMarco (Revell, 2003), *The Dateable Rules: A Guide to the Sexes* (Revell, 2004), and *The Hardest 30 Days of Your Life* (Nelson, 2003).

"Kids will never tell their parents the questions they ask me, and most parents have no idea what's going on with their teens," he says. "I just throw out the information and put it in a way that they understand and enjoy."

For more information on Justin Lookadoo's ministry, visit www.RU-dateable.com. and www.lookadoo.com

Chapter 25

LAUGH IT UP: WRITING WITH HUMOR
Lorilee Craker

*"I firmly believe that, as the cliché goes,
laughter is the shortest distance between two people.
You disarm people when you write in a funny way,
so people begin to listen to what you have to say."*

Lorilee Craker grew up between the shelves of her father's Christian bookstore in Winnipeg, Manitoba. She learned to love books, Christian books especially, in that tiny, inner-city store located next to a massage parlor and across the street from a disco.

Her book-filled childhood naturally fed her love for writing. Teachers complimented her writing skills in high school, but it wasn't until college at Moody Bible Institute in Chicago that her journalism professor suggested she could write for a living.

"I took him at his word because there was nothing else I ever wanted to do. Writing is the only thing I'm really good at, so it's worked out quite well," says Craker.

She has written seven nonfiction books, all with her signature twist of humor that has readers laughing and crying at the same time. Her first was *A is for Adam: Biblical Baby Names*; her most recent is *We Should Do This More Often: A Parents' Guide to Romance, Passion, and Other Prechild Activities You Vaguely Recall*. Her titles also include *When the Belly Button Pops the Baby's Done*, *See How They Run*, and *Just a Little Piece of Quiet*.

"Humor is everywhere," says Craker. "It's best to laugh at what you can't change."

Which explains Lorilee's books on pregnancy ("an absolute treasure trove of humor"), baby's first year, toddlers, preschoolers, and sex ("the number one source of humor.")

Comedy is Hard   Writing with humor isn't as easy as it sounds. Lorilee remembers hearing a speaker say that Christians who can write humorously are the "chosen few of the chosen few" because it's so difficult to find the right tone, choose the right words, and tap into the best vein of laughs.

"I firmly believe that, as the cliché goes, laughter is the shortest distance between two people," says Craker. "You disarm people when you write in a funny way, and in doing so people begin to listen to what you have to say."

But how do you summon up the snickers, snorts, and belly laughs that can bridge that gap between you and your readers? Craker offers several suggestions.

First, look for humorous jumping-off points. For Craker, it was her pregnancy, nursing, toddlers, sleep deprivation, potty training, and weird cravings. Kids in general are hilarious. She chose to find the humor in situations that were occasionally disastrous, usually just funny. She cautions, however, that the humor may not be immediately evident.

"Kids can be hilarious, especially toddlers, and you have to laugh because otherwise you're going to cry," she says.

Jumping-off points can include your own calamities of any stripe. Perhaps you neglected to don a piece of clothing, carried part of your lunch between your teeth for the afternoon, or forgot where you parked the car. Old or young, parents, single or empty nesters, everybody's got a story to tell. She also uses the things that drive her crazy as jumping-off points.

"Some kind of disaster happens to everybody. When you make fun of yourself you're very vulnerable, but people are more willing to listen to your message because you don't take yourself too seriously," says Craker.

Second, use the humor of other people as a jumping-off point. Erma Bombeck, Dave Barry, and Julie Barnhill are among Craker's favorite reads when she's feeling a humor drought. She's laughing with them and refilling her humor reservoir as well.

When those droughts come, Craker knows she can always come back and add funny touches to her writing later. This doesn't work, however, for the entertainment writing she does for her local newspaper. Sometimes she settles for a witty word here and there as a quick deadline approaches.

"There's humor in our frailty and in our foibles, and there's even humor when we're suffering," she says. "Like my uncle's funeral, which was a sorrowful event for everybody. I couldn't help but find humor in the fact that the reception was kosher and there were maybe thirty Jewish people and 200 Mennonites, and a Mennonite never met a pig he didn't want to eat. It was disconcerting for them to find no pork."

Craker has been writing humor for almost a decade. She's learned to not force the humor, but to gently prod herself and sometimes come back later to spice up her writing. Piling on the humor can get annoying as well she's learned, which takes away from the rhythm of the book. Too much humor doesn't give people a chance to breathe.

Second, she tells writers to write what makes them laugh. Remember, though, that what makes you howl can be as dull as dirt for other people.

"I remember my husband at the film *O Brother, Where Art Thou?* He was practically falling in the aisle and tears were running down his face. I'm sitting there saying, 'I don't get this. This is sort of funny, but I'm not dying here.'"

Also, don't take yourself too seriously, which according to Craker is the worst thing you can do.

"It absolutely amazes me that people can write about absurd things in a completely serious way. They can't find it in themselves to make fun of what is clearly absurd, like when I was researching breast feeding and came across this deathly serious sentence about how a mother's milk tea that increases your milk flow could also make you smell like maple syrup. I just laughed and laughed, then made fun of it in my book."

Writing humor does have its limits, however. She had to tone down her list of "Top 10 Baby Gross-Outs" thanks to the fine line between funny and gross. Humor should also never include racial jokes or slurs, and anything that might be construed as mean (except to those oversensitive types who never laugh anyway). Lastly, avoid perfectionism. Writers who want perfection are too high strung to really write humorously anyway.

"I think the key is to just try to have fun with what you write," says Craker. "It's hard to write humor, but if you've got a jumping-off point and you're not too hard on yourself you can make a good start."

Excerpt from *O, for a Thousand Nights to Sleep:*

It was one of those 'aye yi yi' moments indelibly en-
graved on my consciousness. I joined a gym and, as part
of the membership deal, was able to spend an hour with a
personal-trainer type to 'assess' my bod, evaluating exactly
what needed to happen for said bod to get buff. Of course,
I had the wrong shoes, right off the bat. Having never been
much of a workout fiend, I didn't own any shoes that were
remotely right for exercising. So there I was, wearing baggy
sweats and these vaguely sneakery-looking things (I think
they were suede) and bracing myself for the perky chick
with the ripped abs to put me through my paces.

"Hi, I'm Mike. I'm going to be doing your fitness evaluation today."

Gulp. He had ripped abs all right, but he wasn't fe-
male. In fact, before me stood one of God's gifts to wom-
ankind, a guy so dazzling I could barely speak. (You know
by now I'm happily married, and I love Doyle dearly. What
I'm telling you ladies is, this guy was amazing, and anyone,
even a contented matron such as myself, would have been
unhinged by this person's attractiveness. You know Tom
Cruise? Getting warmer.)

"Oh," I managed, peeking again at my ridiculous foot-
wear and decidedly unhip clothing. It was going to take all
my poise—and I've never had much—to get through the
next hour with Mr. Perfection.

"Get a grip, girl! This is a fitness professional, after
all. He's probably seen flabbier than you in his day" was
my pep talk to myself. Of course, as I cast a furtive glance
around, there seemed to be only Victoria's Secret mod-
els and 21-year-old tennis scholarship recipients prancing
around. So much for that … .

My cheeks now a shade somewhere between mango
pink and eggplant purple, I underwent a series of mortify-
ing toning exercises, under Mike's dutiful tutelage.
Then this amazon man/instructor of the very hideous "fire
hydrant" exercise kindly inquired if I was also interested in
weight loss as part of my goals as a new gym member.

Well, yeah. Duh!

"It's been harder than usual to lose weight," I confided. "Ever since the birth of my son."

"Of course," Mike crooned sympathetically. "After all, you just had a baby."

Yeah, twenty-six months ago! He must have thought I said my baby was two months old, not two years old.

"Right! Absolutely! Yes! You are right!" I said enthusiastically. After all, why in the world would I disabuse this nice fellow of his mistaken notion? This way, I could leave, a little sweatier, more rosy-cheeked, and still wearing ludicrous shoes, yet with a fiber of dignity still intact. I had had a baby recently! Which explained—yeah, rationalized—my additional *avoirdupois*. What a break! (p.115)

Chapter 26

Jean Syswerda
WORDS AND THE WORD
Jean Syswerda

*"You don't just study Scripture and then leave;
you study Scripture and leave changed."*

Jean Syswerda knows the power of the Word and the power of words. Her work over the years has often involved putting together innovative Bibles and Bible studies. During her years at Zondervan, Syswerda was instrumental in creating the *NIV Adventure Bible*, the *Women's Devotional Bible*, the *NIV Teen Study Bible*, and the *NIV Youth Walk Devotional Bible*.

Syswerda is now a freelance writer and editor, yet she finds herself as immersed in Bibles and Bible studies as ever. Her first two writing projects as a freelancer were the study titled *Women of the Bible* and the *Women of Faith Study Bible*.

"If somebody had told me ten years ago that I would be sitting at a desk every day writing, I would have thought they were absolutely out of their minds," laughs Syswerda. "I'm too much of a people person."

Syswerda has continued to work on special Bible projects for Zondervan and other publishers while developing her expertise in writing Bible studies. She created an 8-book series called Mom's Ordinary Day, and she's working on another. For *Women of the Bible* she wrote fifty-two brief Bible studies, one for each biblical woman featured in the book.

She offers this advice for writing Bible studies for publication:

1. Find an innovative idea. Syswerda encourages would-be authors to find a new audience, new subject, or new approach.

"If it's already been published, there's no point in you doing it again," she says. "Try to find a fresh approach, a different way of looking at Scripture, or a different group of people that has not been specifically written for before."

2. Know your audience. "A writer must continually keep in mind who her audience is. When I was doing the Mom's Ordinary Day Bible studies I always kept in mind that I was speaking to moms who were at home full-time or at least part-time, had time to go to a Bible study, and so had a particular set of needs that were different from, say, a mom who worked full-time and had her kids in daycare or a mom whose kids were already out of the house."

3. Look at Scripture in a new way. Syswerda's goal in each study is to look at a passage of Scripture, its foundation and background, then provide bits of information and insight that readers wouldn't ordinarily know.

"I want to give people something fresh, then build inspiration from there. I don't want to stop at just teaching, because intellectual knowledge isn't going to help anybody," she says. "Learning needs to go beyond knowledge. You don't just study Scripture and then leave; you study Scripture and leave changed."

4. Ask readers questions to help them think and respond. She learned this lesson through creating studies for *Women of the Bible.* Her editor pushed her to ask the right questions in the right way. That means questions to make readers process information, not just record it. Processing allows participants to work through the Scripture, their own biases or lack of knowledge, and move to a scripturally-based conclusion.

"It's figuring out what will draw people out rather than simply inform them. It's all in how you frame the questions," says Syswerda.

"I also have to frame questions in such a way that users can find the answer or give an opinion. I can't say, 'What's the meaning of this Hebrew word?' You can't expect them to have the resources to find the answer."

Bible studies often include a reader's guide, which lists answers to the questions. When answers are available this adds a new dimension of challenge to the writer's task of framing questions.

"My goal is to bring people knowledge to help them respond, but without telling them how they have to respond."

5. Acknowledge the work of the Holy Spirit. The Holy Spirit plays a large role in Syswerda's work. Often she wonders where her words came from, where the idea for a section began.

"I think, for Christian writers, especially those writing something they hope the Holy Spirit will use in people's lives, it's important to start from what God wants to say through you instead of starting from your own ability. I have people who pray with me through a project, and I certainly pray over my work."

When asked where she thinks the market for Bibles is going, Syswerda replies, "I think as long as people feel longing and emptiness or something lacking in their lives, there will be a good market for Bibles. People sense that the answers come from some place beyond themselves and Scripture is one of those places to get answers. But does that mean there is room for more and different kinds of Bibles? I can't answer that. Today there is so much out there; just about every way you can slice or dice it has been done. It's not a bad thing for there to be lots of different types of Bibles. But I also don't think you can expect success every time you put one out."

BEST SELLER TIP

Writing Journey

Jean Syswerda worked as a waitress between sessions of college. One day she waited on one of her college professors who was having lunch with a friend who worked for the Christian Reformed Church youth program called Young Calvinists. She learned that their magazine, *Insight,* was short an editorial assistant. Jean applied for the job and ended up working for the magazine for five years, eventually becoming assistant editor. After her first child was born, Jean worked as a freelance writer, editor, and proofreader for a variety of publishers, including Zondervan. Zondervan invited her to freelance in-house on a special project; she never really left. She eventually became an associate publisher. Syswerda left Zondervan to restart her freelance career in the late 1990s.

BEST SELLER TIP

Five Keys to Writing Effective Bible Studies

1. Find an innovative idea.

2. Know your audience.

3. Look at Scripture in a new way.

4. Ask questions that will make readers think and respond.

5. Acknowledge the work of the Holy Spirit.

Chapter 27

Ami McConnell and Laura Jensen Walker

THE SCOOP ON CHICK LIT

Ami McConnell and Laura Jensen Walker

"The uniqueness of Christian chick lit is that it takes into account the spiritual life of the protagonist. She's walking in faith, which factors into all the other decisions she makes. Just because she has faith doesn't mean she's effective in all those areas, but faith is a consideration."

WestBow Press editor Ami McConnell is a professional woman, a wife, mother of young children, and the ultimate juggler. Maybe that's why chick lit titles such as *Dreaming in Black and White* and *Dreaming in Technicolor* by Laura Jensen Walker appeal to her.

"Chick lit feels real to me as a modern woman," says McConnell, who edited Walker's books. "There are things that contemporary literature does for our spirit and mind that are necessary and good and edifying, but chick lit answers the question, 'Is life as funny as it looks?'

"My life may be sort of a mess, but chick lit says that's okay and great and authentic, and it gives readers an outlet for that sense of the frenetic in their lives."

Walker's novel features Phoebe Grant, a thirty-something single who dreams of writing more than obituaries at the newspaper. When the movie critic job opens up, Phoebe hopes for a chance but ends up being fired. She heads back to her hometown, only to find Alex Spencer, the man who fired her, there as well.

Phoebe personifies what chick lit is all about: a sassy, single woman struggling to keep the many aspects of her life afloat.

"A chick lit protagonist, often single, will struggle in her career, love relationships, family relationships and friendships," says McConnell. "The chick lit protagonist is constantly wrestling with all these areas at once."

It's that element of authenticity first seen in *Bridget Jones' Diary*, often credited with being one of the first books in the genre, that appeals to women who are thrilled to learn other women are as stressed as they are.

"It's the first time in contemporary literature that we've admitted that we're all making a mess of it," says McConnell.

"It's real," says Walker. "These novels where the heroine is drop-dead gorgeous and brilliant and has a wonderful man and a perfect life: Come on! We get caught up in the trap of trying to be what we think we're supposed to be, but hopefully we've grown up and women are being a little more real today."

Looking Honestly at Faith, Womanhood Christian publishing houses stepped up quickly behind the secular houses to produce their own version of chick lit. Authors such as Kristin Billerbeck, Robin Jones Gunn, Walker, and others are offering Christian readers a pretty honest look at womanhood and faith.

"The uniqueness of Christian chick lit is that it takes into account the spiritual life of the protagonist. She's walking in faith, which factors into all the other decisions she makes," says McConnell. "Just because she has faith doesn't mean she's effective in all those areas, but faith is a consideration."

Another key aspect of chick lit is humor. In secular chick lit that humor can be biting, sarcastic, and mean. Walker hopes her humor never becomes mean, but she's certainly sassy and sarcastic. The humor side of chick lit was no trouble for her. After publishing ten humorous nonfiction books, she knew how to draw a laugh. What she didn't know how to do was write a novel.

It was the Mount Hermon writers' conference that gave her the nudge she needed. First was Davis Bunn's seminar on writing fiction. He told his audience that before a writer begins a novel, she should have an idea how it ends. Well, she did have an ending. Then Laura attended a panel discussion featuring top fiction editors from every major house. When she asked if they were looking for humor, everyone said yes, then one added, "If you can write it. Most people can't."

"It was like God said, 'See? I gave you the gift of humor. This will be your bridge from nonfiction to fiction.' Afterward I sat down and wrote the opening line and the next line, and the novel just flowed."

Chick lit and its various permutations resonate with women regardless of age and marital status, whether young moms or empty nesters, wealthy or not. There's hen lit (for slightly older and perhaps married women), mom lit, chick lit that appeals to women of diversity, and books that appeal to the older generation.

"It's harder for us to read up, to identify with a stage we haven't reached, but if we've been there already we can identify with the protagonist," says McConnell. "If the repartee is there, if the sense of not taking life too seriously is there, we get it and it sounds authentic to us."

Chick Lit's Future Looks Bright   It's difficult to predict where reader interest and trends will turn even six months ahead, but McConnell thinks chick lit may not have reached its peak yet. She's interested in chick lit about women in different stages of life, in different socioeconomic places. This diversity will fuel the chick lit genre.

"I think as women we're intrigued by people who are very different from us, so I think we'll start seeing more chick lit that involves protagonists who are less like us," says McConnell.

Chick lit allows women a unique, sassy voice that has often been constrained in order to make it more acceptable. Artistic constraints kept women's voices muted, but thematic constraints did as well. Certain topics were taboo, as was a protagonist who spoke her mind and showed her flaws. Women writers now feel free to write authentically.

"I think a lot of women have been liberated not only in terms of their voice artistically but also in terms of theme. They're free to write about people who are very flawed, very imperfect. It's also spiritually liberating to see protagonists who are struggling," says McConnell.

Phoebe Grant has her flaws to be sure. She's occasionally selfish, jumps to conclusions, and spends too much money on shoes. But she's also kindhearted and loves God and her family.

"I want Phoebe flawed because that's what people relate to," says Walker.

For Walker, one of the most difficult things about writing Christian chick lit is avoiding being preachy. She wants the Christian message in there, but not in-your-face. It's also difficult to balance humor and story.

"The pace of your humor cannot be too breakneck for the reader," she says. "You have to give them a little pause and a time to catch their breath. It's important to know when to stop."

Is there room for similar books for men? A little lad lit out there?

"I don't think so," replies McConnell. "Men are less interested in how to balance all these aspects of life; they're much more linear in thinking. Women want to consider all aspects of a situation, but men want to get right to the point, find the killer, or solve the crime."

Walker adds, "Chick lit is girlfriend stuff. It's like talking to your girlfriends, and that's why it's so popular."

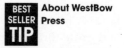
BEST SELLER TIP **About WestBow Press**

WestBow Press is the publisher of all fiction previously released by Nelson Books and W Publishing Group. Launched in 2003, WestBow's authors include Ted Dekker, Angela Hunt, Frank Peretti and Davis Bunn. WestBow is named after the street in Edinburgh, Scotland, called West Bow, where Thomas Nelson launched his publishing company in 1798.

For more information on WestBow Press, visit www.thomasnelson.com. For information on Laura Jensen Walker's other books and upcoming releases, visit www.laurajensenwalker.com. For further discussion on Christian chick lit, visit www.faithfulreader.com/features/.

Chapter 28

Ted Olsen

WRITING FOR
ONLINE PUBLICATIONS
Ted Olsen

"In a magazine or newspaper, readers are drawn by a headline,
a deck, a picture and caption, sometimes a call-out
all on the same page. But online you may only have
a headline to grab a reader, so it must be very clear.
It doesn't have to be boring, but it should be explanatory."

T ed Olsen is the online managing editor for *Christianity Today*. He develops, assigns, edits, and places content for the Web version of the popular Christian magazine, a separate entity under the ChristianityToday.com umbrella. He uses content from the other ten magazines under that umbrella, but his work is specifically for CT's online publication.

Olsen has been building the magazine's online presence since 1999. Through the years he's learned there are similarities and differences between online writing and writing for the print media, such as newspapers and magazines.

"The most important similarity is that good writing is good writing, whether for online or print publications," says Olsen. "You also need to know the publication you're writing for and exactly what the editor wants."

Writers often believe that online writing is more personal, less objective. Not true, according to Olsen. Straight news stories are just as important online as ever.

"The blogging phenomenon has created a community that believes all the rules of writing objectively have changed. Wrong. You still write articles on assignment like you do for print outlets," he says.

The skills are the same: Research the market, present a strong query and clips, find out exactly what your editor wants, write to topic and length, meet deadlines, know your audience, and write well.

It comes down to intentionality, according to Olsen. "You need to know what you're writing and who you're writing for. An article you write for ChristianityToday.com should be totally different from what you write for Christianwoman.com."

Different Needs, Different Styles There are differences between online and print writing, as well. One is an increased need for tight writing. While some gurus say to cut print writing by 50 percent to make it work online, Olsen says that might be extreme. The issue, he says, is eliminating the extras.

"You need to put the important things at the top of your article. You don't always need to write in the old Associated Press inverted pyramid style for online work, but you'd better have the important stuff in the first three or four paragraphs."

Online readers are sold on an article according to what they see on that first screen. People aren't often willing to scroll to look for the point of your article, so make it early and make it clearly. Olsen describes changing writers' leads to make sure readers know right away what the article is about.

Online readers are often scanners, he says. They scan a page quickly, so whatever catches the eye must be clear and concise. That makes headlines paramount. For ChristianityToday.com, that means a headline such as "Missionaries Killed in Iran" instead of "Terror on Terror."

"In a magazine or newspaper, readers are drawn by a headline, a deck, a picture and caption, sometimes a callout all on the same page. But online you may only have a headline to grab a reader, so it must be very clear. It doesn't have to be boring, but it should be explanatory," says Olsen.

The second and third paragraphs also take on new meaning in online writing, according to Olsen. Because readers assume that the first paragraph is a restating of the headline, they skip to later paragraphs for new information.

"That's why I say the first screen is much more important than the first paragraph. The second and third paragraphs are more important online because a lot of readers come into the story on them."

Online readers tend to look quickly over a page to see what catches their eye. Write, therefore, with scanners in mind. Use bulleted lists, boldface type, tables and charts, and subheads.

"A lot of us writers like to show off our prose abilities, so we don't like to write in bulleted lists. We find it to be a bit too pedestrian," says Olsen. "But writers need to ask themselves if the information could be presented in a table or list."

Broader Audience, More Critics Another difference is that online writing lends itself to being taken out of context far more easily than print writing. Scanners may miss the irony of an article, miss a transition that is key to later points, may gloss over a change in perspective. Also, online audiences are much broader than most print outlets. This means more casual readers and more critics.

An article you write on music for your denominational magazine may not be controversial to your readers, but someone doing a casual Google search on the topic may come to your article with an opposite perspective. Maybe they'll be outraged, write you letters, harangue your theology.

"You have to have thicker skin if you're writing online," Olsen contends, "and you also have to write with the understanding that people are going to disagree with you more than they would in a print context. Some people go out and look for things to criticize. One problem with the blogosphere is that it's become so easy to criticize anything."

Online websites are very easy to access from anywhere in the world. Olsen says that 20 percent of ChristianityToday.com readers are from outside the United States. Writers must be careful of pop culture allusions that foreign readers won't understand. Olsen doesn't recommend cutting all such references, but to realize that 10-to-20 percent of potential readers aren't going to understand. It's a good idea to explain idioms and jargon, and to make your perspective on a topic clear and strong.

Generating traffic at a website with controversial or exciting articles is one thing, but building an audience is another, says Olsen. Advertisers love to have lots of potential buyers visiting lots of pages, but marketing folks like visitors to stay forever, to bookmark the site or make it a home page.

That's why he looks for articles that do both, but adds "It's a main course versus dessert kind of thing. The traffic generators are our dessert, but the bulk of our articles have to be the meat-and-potatoes stuff that people come to the website for."

Another difference is an issue of trust. Online content, according to Olsen, has a far lower trust factor than print media, in part because anybody can pass themselves off as an expert, but also because sites such as Amazon.com provide book reviews written by people with a vested interest in promoting a product.

"That's not going to happen in print," says Olsen. "There's a lot of online marketing content trying to pass itself off as objective; there's a lot of spin out there. So recognize there's a chance you won't be trusted."

Proofreading and Checking Facts   Proofreading your original work is also a must when writing online. Online editors move quickly, don't have as many editors reading the piece, don't have time to carefully proofread each item. It's important, also, to check your sources, because online editors aren't going to.

"People aren't going to trust you if they see a lot of proofreading errors," cautions Olsen.

The biggest thing that separates print media and online writing, however, is links. Links can bring readers to ancillary articles or research or other websites that augment the topic, but just as often links can burden a reader when overused.

"Link only important things that are directly related to what you're writing," says Olsen. He cautions against links easily found on Google (offer your readers something unique), links to broad sites instead of specific articles or reviews (the one you want may be too hard to find), and links that may not be operating when the article is published (newspaper articles, for instance.) He recommends posting newspaper and other articles right on your site instead of linking to another site.

Online writing isn't going away any time soon. Despite the growth of blogging, good reporting is still needed.

"There's a crazy lack of good reporting online," says Olsen. "If you can report, your editor will love you. Look for something unique and do some reporting instead of doing something that's just off the top of your head. I'm always looking for the story."

The Scoop on Subheads
by Ann Byle

Whenever I write a longer article for a newspaper or magazine, I always include my own subheads. I know the article's natural transitions, which are great spots for subheads, as well as where the article may become heavy with necessary information. Subheads not only give the reader a visual break, but can also draw them into reading what follows.

I've also found that many editors include those subheads in the final product. Because this has happened so often, I think pretty seriously about each subhead. Often editors are thrilled that they don't have to come up with subheads.

"The writer who can actually think in terms of subheads is rare," confirms Ted Olsen.

He looks specifically for breaking news, but also for what he calls evergreen topics: timeless stories that will stay around a good long while, like online writing itself.

For news and information, visit www.ChristianityToday.com.

Chapter 29

ACT ONE: LEARNING THE ART OF SCREENWRITING
Barbara Nicolosi

*"Hollywood needs primarily one thing
and that is story. There is room for anyone
who is passionate and really works hard
and brings something to the table."*

Barbara Nicolosi dreams of Christian writers, producers, directors, and actors bringing faith into Hollywood, one person at a time. She envisions professionals at all levels of movie and television production companies helping create highest quality material that points people to issues of truth, love, and faith.

Her dream is becoming reality, thanks to Act One, Inc., the nonprofit organization she founded in 1999 to train people of faith for careers in mainstream Hollywood.

"We are trying to create a community of Christian professionals for the entertainment industry who will motivate each other to live godly and very creative lives. These people will be each others' best friends professionally and spiritually," says Nicolosi.

Act One began by offering a month-long intensive screenwriting program designed to teach the basics. The rigor of "Writing for Hollywood" does several things: It teaches, it shows participants what real life in Hollywood is like, and it weeds out those writers who find that screenwriting isn't for them. Nicolosi estimates about 20 percent of those who complete the program make this decision. She accepts thirty of the approximately 300 applications she receives for each session.

"The program was originally conceived as a boot camp experience, but what happened was that alumni of the program started asking for more help," says Nicolosi. "They wouldn't go away. Now the boot camp is a doorway into Act One."

Its newest step is the Entertainment Internship & Executive Training Program, a 12-week summer event designed to train and mentor Christians who will eventually make decisions as top executives in Hollywood. They are working on similar programs for producers and actors. Act One also offers weekend seminars around the country, website resources, a critique service, alumni events, mentorships, and even a bit of career counseling.

"When we tell someone that in our view they're in the wrong career, we do that with very serious reflection because we know the ramifications. We feel that we owe it to them," says Nicolosi.

The Act One programs center on four key areas where Nicolosi feels Christians fall behind in Hollywood: artistry, professionalism, content, and spirituality. Each class or program Act One offers is centered on these four areas, as well as on hands-on learning.

Christians are Missing the Boat   Nicolosi has some pretty good ideas why Christians aren't playing a more prominent role in Hollywood. Some of the reasons are the same as why non-Christians don't make it. Others are less obvious.

"This is a tremendously demanding arena. You have to be very self motivated and very disciplined because people don't give you millions of dollars for your stuff if it isn't good," Nicolosi says. "I think a lot of Christians have no respect for how hard it is."

The twentysomethings she's seeing these days are so in love with Hollywood, so enamored with the glitz and glamour, that they think it'll be easy: that making it in Hollywood is a matter of sitting on the beach, working a bit, and being adopted by someone terribly famous.

"We tell them to forget that. If you want to work forty hours a week, don't come to Hollywood because no one works forty hours a week here. You're playing with the big boys now," says Nicolosi. "You have to be up for very demanding, very creative, very hard work."

Christians also tend to mix up the messages of Hollywood with the craft of Hollywood. Because the message is skewed, Christians think the craft is bad.

Wrong, says Nicolosi. Bad craft is bad whether its Christ-based or not.

"You might be farther along spiritually, but that doesn't mean you are a good artist and it certainly doesn't mean that you're competitive. There are a lot of people who make wonderful, very well executed things, but they're pagans. For some Christians, being able to respect that and understand the difference is a big thing. Humility is the first thing you must have to learn anything."

Christians, just like any other writers in Hollywood, must have talent. That talent is more than writing witty dialogue or great action scenes. It's learning that screenwriting is a multilevel art form. Nicolosi talks of the levels of meaning in each screenplay. There are poetic images, dialogue, scene descriptions, the musical and other background sound effects, and the actors' performances.

"It's a very complex art," she says. "Most writers, especially those who don't come to Act One, are thinking of a movie as talking heads. Their movies tend to be chatty and focused on witty conversation, but that's not what makes a good movie."

Networking is Key   Networking is huge in Hollywood. It's all about who you know, who knows you, who trusts you. Act One is a great place to build that network. Nicolosi repeatedly sees the benefits of a strong network.

"We help create their first group of people they know who will either lead to jobs for them or give them their first credits. The good thing is, these are like-minded people," she says.

Those credits perhaps gained through an Act One network are vital. Writers must be able to show that they have done the work and done it well.

"That line from the Bible—'… those who are faithful in little things will be entrusted with bigger ones'—is never so true as it is in Hollywood," says Nicolosi. "You have to show that you have done a lot of little things well before people will trust you with bigger jobs.

"The guild rate to write a screenplay is $70,000. No one is going to give you that for your first screenplay. Getting that experience is what everyone is trying to do. They're trying to get credits, to be seen, to get their first shot. But there really is no first shot; there are many shots."

Avoiding the   The kiss of death in Hollywood is getting a
'Difficult' Label reputation for being difficult. While actors may get away with it, writers can't.

"People in Hollywood will work with someone not as talented who can do the job before they'll work with somebody who is difficult," says Nicolosi.

The inability to make compromises, missing deadlines, writing badly, not doing research, and promising something you can't deliver are enough to end your career. Christians, however, seem to have the corner on being whiny, complainy, and paranoid.

"That's because Christians too often turn everything into a God issue. The fact is, most of them aren't," says Nicolosi.

She describes the many Christians who tell her that God told them to write a certain movie script. Sure, she says, the idea may be good, but the writer says it has to be set in 1947 when in reality it doesn't. The issue then becomes a matter of fidelity to God.

"That makes us sound like nuts. Most of the changes people make in scripts are not to annoy the Christian right. Most changes are because people are trying to save money. A lot of Christians aren't up for that," says Nicolosi.

Playing the   After living and working in Hollywood for
God-Told-Me Card   so many years, Nicolosi has seen it all. She's
                       experienced the sublime and the ridiculous.
But it's the Christians who sit in her office and tell her she can't touch their horribly written scripts because "God is the one who dictated this to me" that really irk her.

"I say, 'I would have thought God was a better writer than that,'" she says. "We joke about people telling us 'You have to help me because God told me you're the one,' because we've all heard it so many times. Well, God didn't mention it to me."

One of the problems she faced when starting Act One was that Christians already established in the industry were afraid to work with the program because they'd been burned so many times before by self-righteous Christians demanding their services only because they are Christians. Act One policy is to never refer a student for a job unless he or she is qualified to do it.

The Deeper Issue   Nicolosi sees an even deeper issue in the clash
                       of Hollywood and Christianity. Hollywood
represents a culture of paganism, materialism, ego, sex, and stardom. Christians demand that this culture make films that promote the truths of God, but it can't. It doesn't know how.

"One of the things I say to Christians who get irate about Hollywood's choices is to look at it from their standpoint. If the situation were reversed and Christians were the ones with all the power, would we feel obliged to make a few porn movies just for the people who like them? But in one sense, that's what Christians are asking Hollywood to do. They're making movies they want to see and we're demanding they make movies we want to see."

But those demands often don't translate into Christians' becoming part of the creative, collaborative process that is Hollywood. The answer lies in Christians' becoming involved at all levels, which is the goal of Act One.

Another area of concern is mediocrity. Christians, according to Nicolosi, tend to allow mediocrity because of our penchant for looking at the heart, not the art.

"The secular side has no compulsion to do that. In Christian art we have so much slop because we're justifying the art based on a person's heart. Christians competing in the secular world are playing for a much higher stake and therefore have a lot more quality checks."

Hollywood takes notice to be sure. When it sees Christians praising mediocre movies only because there was no swearing, a Christian protagonist or nobody slept together, it's confused. When Hollywood sees profound stories of redemption or forgiveness blasted by Christians or ignored, it gives up and makes the mediocre movies the powerful Christian marketplace is willing to see.

"The secular world hears us saying we're profound people who have the Holy Spirit, and then we say we love a movie they know is crap. We're ending up giving a false witness to what our faith is. It's devastating," says Nicolosi.

The answer? The church adopting Hollywood as a mission field and supporting those who go there to work for God from the inside. Supporting organizations such as Act One, whose funding comes from donations. Recognizing that art and artists play a vital role in faith and culture.

"We say to our artists today, 'Go get a real job and then on the side paint the Sistine Chapel.' Michelangelo couldn't paint the Sistine Chapel on the side. He had the church say to him, 'We'll feed you, clothe you, and house you, and you make your beautiful stuff,'" says Nicolosi.

Act One has begun to see its alumni getting jobs as production assistants and writer's assistants, being hired to write scripts, and selling their work. More and more are signing with big Hollywood agencies, a prerequisite for moving up in the ranks, and a few are

A Christian Hollywood Success Story

Clare Sera attended the inaugural "Writing for Hollywood" program in 1999. She came away with a wealth of practical knowledge for surviving and thriving in Hollywood.

"What impressed me was that it was taught by people literally walking off the lots to come teach. It was up-to-the-minute in every aspect," says Sera. "The cool thing was that Act One gave me the confidence that I could pursue screenwriting and not lose my soul to the devil. I needed to know that."

Sera has consulted with another writer on a number of scripts, including one made into the film *Laws of Attraction*. She is also a writer on the script for Universal Studios' feature film *Curious George*.

"At Act One I was given insights that would have taken me a couple of years to figure out on my own," says Clare. "Screenwriting in Hollywood is hard work, and you have to be excellent at your trade. Act One opened my eyes."

working on major-budget movies. Barbara's goal is to grow Act One into a year-round, complete film school for people of faith. It's not about one big movie that changes Hollywood and the world. It's about long-term commitment to changing culture.

"We believe one of the jobs of Christians is to bring God where he is not," says Nicolosi. "So we are very much about placing our students in the middle of the arena of the mainstream. We want our students at Warner Brothers and Paramount and Columbia. We want them on the sets, on the TV shows, and in the offices of the networks and cable shows.

"Our culture is not going to heal itself and it's not going to be healed without the presence of Christians actively giving their voices to it. I think the people of God are starting to see that, and that brings tremendous hope."

For more information on Act One, Inc. programs or funding opportunities, visit www.actoneprogram.com.

Behind the Scenes: Nurturing Writers in the Craft

Chapter 30

Jeanette Thomason

SEARCHING OUT THE BEST WRITERS

Jeanette Thomason

*"Some people will give me a 15-page synopsis.
That's not what I want. I want the nut:
that little blip that grabs you about it."*

Jeanette Thomason has the heart of both an editor and a reader. That makes her a great acquisition editor, a role she has relished at Baker Publishing Group. Her job was to find new talent as well as work with current Baker authors to help them develop book ideas.

"I got to look for great people with great messages and great book ideas," she says.

Her concept of acquisitions has been honed by years in the writing business. She began her career as a journalist working for a number of newspapers as a beat reporter and feature writer. She then moved into magazines, first with *Virtue*, then at *Aspire*. After a brief time at iBelieve.com, she became an acquisition editor at Baker Publishing Group. Thomason worked primarily with the Revell division, actively recruiting both fiction and nonfiction authors.

The search, she says, is constant and ongoing. She find authors in a variety of ways:

1. Writers' conferences, though she's selective about which ones she attends. Those that have been in business for a long time, that are well organized, and that are committed to raising the standards of excellence in writing are the best choices.

"I find people at writers' conferences who are committed to developing their craft," says Thomason.

2. Contacts with creative writing programs. "I like to put feelers out to people who might run across great writing. I say, 'If you see this or this, let me know,' or 'Keep me in mind if you come across this type of fiction.'"

3. Reading. Thomason reads writers' magazines, literary magazines such *Glimmer Train* and *The Atlantic* and others, as well as popular magazines such as *Today's Christian Woman* and *People.*

"My antenna is always up. I'm always trying to think of connections, of who has something interesting to say. I like to match up unlikely people or people with unlikely situations, and have them say something surprising," she says. "Like my old crusty newspaper editor used to say, 'It's not news if there's not a twist.' I look for the twist when I look for books."

4. The slush pile. Thomason found Ray Blackston, author of *Flabbergasted, A Delirious Summer* and *Lost in Rooville,* in the pile of unsolicited manuscripts.

Blackston, she says, exhibited exactly the characteristics she looks for in a new writer. While she liked his voice and style, there were trouble spots.

"There were some issues with his manuscript, which I wrote and told him about. I told him that if he reworked some of these things I would love to see the manuscript again. I didn't make any promises," she recalls. "He reworked exactly the things I'd identified. He didn't have experience, but he did have talent."

Finding the Fresh Voice Thomason is looking for that fresh new voice, that fresh perspective on even an age-old topic. "I ask what makes a manuscript different, what compels me to read it, what's new?" she says.

In book proposals, Thomason wants prospective authors to be able to give her a brief synopsis of the book, then tell her in one page who the main characters are.

"You can always tell a writer's understanding of audience by how he or she does that," she says. "Some people will give me a 15-page synopsis. That's not what I want. I want the nut: that little blip that grabs you about it."

She likens that nut to how you would summarize a movie you've just seen for a friend as you sit in a coffee shop. It's a quick summary that reduces the plot to its barest. Her next step is reading the first chapter. That first chapter tells her how a writer handles language and dialogue, how he tells a story, if he knows how to frame a scene and handle point of view. She can tell almost immediately if she's willing to read on.

"Part of what we do in acquisitions is science and part of it is magic," she says with a laugh.

The science is looking at the craft: point of view, dialogue, active or passive voice, how the story moves, the message. The magic is intuition: talent, what makes a good story, what makes a good storyteller. Thomason guesses the ratio may be half science, half magic.

"There's also the element of creating a great book and doing all the right marketing, but the book doesn't sell. Or you can put a book out there with very little marketing but something happens—the magic part—and the book starts spreading like wildfire," she says.

Understanding the magic also means understanding trends, where an author fits in culture and history, and what's important to readers. It's an iffy business to be sure.

"I have really good days and really bad days," she says.

Time, Thomason says, is an acquisition editor's greatest resource. Using that time wisely doesn't mean always getting to the slush pile, getting to every writers' conference, taking every phone call, or answering every e-mail. It means becoming part of the huge investment a publishing company makes in every book, which can be between $30,000 and $60,000.

Asking the Right Questions

Asking questions is a big part of both an author's and an acquisition editor's life. For a fiction writer, the clichéd but perfect question is "What if?"

What if an active, elderly woman is faced with the prospect of losing her driver's license?

What if a lovely artist moves in next door to a bachelor priest?

What if a single man on the lookout for a wife decides to start trolling at church?

What if a woman has a vision about a murder about to take place?

Another question begging to be asked is "What's eternal here?"

BEST SELLER TIP

Maximize Your Meetings with an Acquisition Editor

Appointments with an acquisition editor during writers' conferences usually last about fifteen minutes. Come prepared to describe what you want to write and why, and who you think needs to read it.

"I want writers to have those things defined very clearly," says acquisitions editor Jeanette Thomason.

Fiction writers should go beyond just having a great story to tell.

"It sounds rough, but the first question is, 'Who cares?' or 'So what?'" she adds. "I want them to respond with 'I think this is an important story because ...' or 'It has to be told because ...'"

"I think new writers and experienced writers need to be examining that question. I don't think everything has to be this dramatic piece of literature that's going to last for ages, but what would happen if every writer asked that question?," says Thomason. "What better writers and acquisition editors we would all be if we measured books by asking, 'Is there anything eternal here to take away?'"

Another question for writers is "What kind of writer am I?" Perhaps your talent lies in profound and insightful work, but you're trying to make everything funny. Maybe you're one of the few who can use humor well, but you're trying to make everything serious. Practice, says Thomason, is key. Scheduled daily or even weekly writing time helps you develop your voice and your skills.

A final question to ask is "What can I do to get my book out there?" As an acquisition editor, Thomason sees the team effort it takes to get a book from idea to manuscript to finished product. The publisher sees that book as a great product and is willing to do its part to get the word out. The other side of the coin is that the author has to be just as excited and persistent.

"I think that sometimes being an acquisition editor is like being one of those judges on the television program *American Idol*. People come to you with their dreams, but you know they have to earn those dreams. They have to have talent and skill and the sense about how to use those things," she says.

"An author must be the evangelist for his or her book."

Visit Baker Publishing Group at www.bakerpublishinggroup.com.

Just before this book went to press, Jeanette Thomason made the move to editorial director at WaterBrook Press, a division of Random House.

Chapter 31

Marking Up More Than a Manuscript
Dave Lambert

*"My feeling is that the editor is probably
the most dedicated reader the author will ever have.
We read those books with a scrutiny and an appreciation
that in all likelihood no other reader is going to have."*

D ave Lambert is the consummate editor. He has years of experience as an acquiring editor for Zondervan. He has guided numerous writers from their eager beginnings into mature, even bestselling, authors. He shares his craft at writers' conferences and has written nine books—fiction and nonfiction—himself.

Now, as a freelance editor, he works with a number of publishing houses and a variety of authors, some of whom insist that he edit their work. His long, pointed manuscript critiques are nearly legendary among the top tier of Christian authors.

This chapter is divided into three sections: First, Lambert's editing process; second, what editors expect from authors; and finally, what authors can expect from an editor.

Manuscript Completed, Editing Begins Lambert begins with this statement: "My assumption is that every author wants the best book he or she can get."

It's also true, he says, that publishing houses want the best book. Everyone's interests are served in creating the best book possible: The publishing house sells books, the author develops a loyal fan base that wants more books, the author grows as a writer who brings more books to the publishing house, which is happy to sell them. The editor's role, then, is crucial.

"My feeling is that the editor is probably the most dedicated reader the author will ever have. We read those books with a scrutiny and an appreciation that in all likelihood no other reader is going to have," he says.

He carefully considers all the key aspects of good fiction. First is characterization. Do a character's actions make sense? Are the main characters likable? Does the character grow and change by the end of the book?

"Every author has a plot in mind, and they want to move their characters through that plot. But what if the character they've created doesn't fit neatly into that plot? It's actually a common problem," he says.

Lambert also looks carefully at the plot. How is the pacing? Does it take too long for the main conflict to really kick in? Is the plot too complex or too simple?

"Novels are great sprawling beasts. Plots have to be relatively complex; if it's too neat it probably belongs in a short story or novella," Lambert says.

Dialogue can also be a problem. Change is necessary if all characters speak in the same voice, use the same number of words, figures of speech, and vocabulary.

"We each have unique voices. Some people speak as if they've planned everything ahead of time, some never use more than three or four words in any sentence. Some speak rarely, others use regional dialect, others as if they've been to finishing school. If these people all sound the same to me, then I'll probably know how the author sounds," he says.

Authors can also write too much dialogue, use too many words.

"Dialogue is an approximation of real speech. If it were real speech nobody could understand it," Lambert says.

Point of view is also a critical area of concern.

"Point of view, for being one of the most basic techniques of fiction, is probably the one that is least grasped by novelists," he says.

Writers want omniscient point of view, but often they don't establish that early in the novel. They jump in and out of characters' heads with reckless abandon, jump points of view when it suits. And it's not a problem just with novice writers. Even the most established writers, inside and outside the Christian publishing industry, have trouble with point of view.

After a close read of the manuscript, Lambert compiles his list of questions and errors to be fixed. He sends off the often lengthy letter and waits. He's gotten such letters himself, so he knows the emotions that flow when an author reads his or her critique.

"First they think I'm wrong, then they think I'm rude. They set it aside for a couple of days, then come back and grudgingly admit that maybe I did a good job reading the manuscript and found some real problems that need to be addressed," he reveals. "Most of the time I'll get back a revised manuscript after a couple of months in which the author really did try to address most of what I pointed out."

Occasionally an author prepares a point-by-point rebuttal to his critiques, which Lambert most often finds to be an excuse for not fixing things. He's occasionally had to send a manuscript back for a second, third, or fourth rewrite.

"In fiction, writing is everything. You have a story to tell and you have one tool, the words on the page, to get that story across. You're creating a fictional dream world, and you want your readers to inhabit that world so completely that they're not even aware they're reading a book," Lambert says. "But clumsy writing—something goes on too long, something happens they don't understand—takes them out of the book."

An Editor Expects ... The key thing that Lambert, and likely any editor, expects from an author is professionalism. That professionalism shows up in a number of ways. First, an author needs to be lifelong learner, always finding ways to improve her craft. Some authors are content with a certain level of success and knowledge of the craft. Editors, however, are eager to see growth and change.

Professionalism also implies that an author understands that the best books are a collaboration between an editor and author.

"That means they're going to take our suggestions seriously, not only for this manuscript but for career development," Lambert says. "If we tell them to spend more time reading books on craft, they'll do it. If we suggest taking a course to improve a particular aspect of their writing, they do it."

Authors also show their professionalism when they understand their role in promoting their own book.

"The best and most effective promotion on any book is done by the author, not the publishing house. Some people think self promotion is a dirty word, but publishing houses don't think that," Lambert says.

Author Patricia Sprinkle is a good example, he says. She contacts bookstores in areas where she is speaking or teaching. Ahead of time she asks if they would like her to come by for a signing, sign copies of books on the shelves, or mention the bookstore in a radio interview as a place to buy her books. That's good and necessary promotion in Lambert's eyes.

He also expects authors to buy into the real sense of partnership between a writer and a publishing house.

"A lot of authors lose sight of this. All they see is that they spent a year writing this manuscript and no one seems to be treating them with respect. But if you count the number of hours that a publishing house is spending on a manuscript, the number of people who are touching it, its commitment is no less."

Lambert also wants a good relationship with an author. Not best friends maybe, but a good working relationship. Cards at birthdays and Christmas, making time for the editor when he or she is in town. It all boils down to professionalism one more time.

An Author Can Expect … An author with an editor worth anything can expect encouragement in equal amounts with criticism. Gentle criticism?

"Often an editor can seem too blunt, but the truth is that it's going to be very, very difficult for any editor to express criticism in a way that isn't threatening to most authors," he says. "It doesn't matter how gentle he or she is, it's still your baby, it's still personal. A writer should expect criticism and be willing to give the benefit of the doubt on how it's delivered."

Also, an author should expect everything to take longer than planned. From returned phone calls to comments on manuscripts, it all takes time. And in a world where fewer people do more work, it's especially true.

"Staff sizes are smaller, but the number of books is bigger so something has to give, and the editor's sanity is usually it," he says with a chuckle.

Beyond the Christian Market Lambert offers a somewhat surprising piece of advice to writers. He encourages them to look for markets outside the Christian media.

"There's nothing that says a Christian should write only for the Christian media. In fact, there's a lot to say about looking for secular outlets for our work," he says.

One of those is that God calls us to spread the Word to those around us. Not, he says, in hokey books where everyone gets saved but in books that present an overt or covert Christian worldview. Doing so allows authors to reach a different audience, to have another market should their writing dry up or the Christian market slow down.

"There are an awful lot of writers who could write for the secular publishing world and have a much more varied and satisfying career and far wider sphere of influence if they did so," he says.

"Christians love to complain about the secular media—movies, books, television. But I say get involved, get something in those same media that reflects Christian values."

What to Expect from an Editor

1. Encouragement.
An editor will find the good in your writing, as well as encourage your career.

2. Criticism.
It's necessary and usually hurts, but remember that the editor has your book's best interest at heart.

3. Time delays.
Editors are busy people working on more than one project. Cut them some slack.

How to Display Professionalism to an Editor

1. Be a lifelong learner.
Always be looking for ways to improve your writing.

2. Understand collaboration.
Take your editor's suggestions seriously for both your manuscript and career.

3. Work hard at promoting.
Find ways to promote and market your own book.

4. Work in partnership. Understand that your publishing house is investing just as heavily as you are in your book. Work with them.

5. Build a good personal relationship.
Develop a good rapport with your editor.

Chapter 32

Building a Relationship with an Editor

Carol Kent

"When both sides are quick with affirmation and choose not to be hurt when a suggestion is made, it makes the relationship stronger and the writing better."

Carol Kent is a well known speaker and writer who travels the United States and the world sharing her message of faith and her knowledge of public speaking. Her most recent book, *When I Lay My Isaac Down*, is a Gold Medallion Finalist, a winner of the Award of Merit from *Christianity Today*, and winner of the 2005 Christian Retailers Award. She speaks often on the subject of that book: her son's arrest and conviction for the murder of his wife's former husband and the life lessons surrounding that horrific time.

When I Lay My Isaac Down is the seventh book Kent has written for NavPress and the third with her editor, Traci Mullins. These two women are more than writer and editor; they are friends. Building a relationship with an editor is vitally important for creating the best book possible and for personal growth as well.

"Every time I work with Traci I feel like I learn how to be a better writer," says Kent, founder of "Speak Up With Confidence" seminars and author of a book by the same name.

Kent began working with Mullins in 1989, partway through her first NavPress book. That book wasn't progressing as well as Kent wished, so she approached the editorial director about working with another editor. He put Kent in touch with Mullins, who became what Kent calls her "writing mentor."

"She immediately helped me think through what my bottom-line premise was. I had chapter ideas and an overall theme, but I didn't have a framework," says Kent.

Through the years Mullins has taught Kent several key things:

1. Create the framework for a book before writing a word, which prevents much rewriting later.

2. Show, don't tell. As author of nine Bible study guides, Kent was good at creating bullet points, using pertinent Scripture, describing the teaching points, and giving application questions. But she needed to flesh those out with more story.

"Traci knows that readers will visualize the point much better if it's wrapped in a story that illustrates the point," Kent says.

3. Strengthen writing skills. Mullins directed Kent to well written books as examples, and she also taught her through her own editing.

4. Freedom. Kent was afraid to venture beyond basic subject-verb sentences, but Mullins showed her that using phrases, single words, and stream-of-consciousness writing worked as well if done judiciously. This freed Kent to express more completely her complex feelings.

5. Tighten sentences. "In the beginning frequently she did this for me. By the time I got to *When I Lay My Isaac Down* I'd learned how to delete extraneous words and filler phrases," Kent says.

Their relationship has grown over the years, enough to be able to work amicably through editorial questions that could have threatened the relationship. *When I Lay My Isaac Down* was a difficult book for Kent to write. She poured her heartbreak and hope, despair and joy into every page.

"There were times when I felt like it was unfair of her to ask me to give so much to a reader because it was so personal to me," Kent says. "In the chapter on the power of joy, I didn't have an illustration about when I experienced joy during these events. But I added something that was very personal, and I've gotten many letters thanking me for being completely honest. It was also hard for me when she called me on my wanting to paint a more positive picture of my child. She asked very serious questions about what led up to the event that took a man's life and my son's role in that. I wanted him to look more perfect than he was."

One key in a vital writer–editor relationship is the ability of both parties to compromise. The writer must understand that an editor is trying to make the best book possible, while an editor can learn to yield on something a writer feels strongly about.

"There is an inborn respect for an editor of Traci's caliber. I know she's coming up with ideas to make this manuscript better," says Kent.

Kent offers good advice for working with an editor. First, don't be afraid to ask for the editor you want. Publishing houses have to pay an editor anyway, so they might as well pay the editor you would most like to work with.

Then, says Kent, "Build the relationship before you build the manuscript. Take time to ask questions about his or her life. Become a friend." Learning a bit about an editor's life builds that relationship. It also helps a writer remember that an editor is a person with a life outside of his or her manuscript.

Kent is also generous with praise. She often thanks Mullins for her work and expertise, as well as her friendship. She passes along responses from readers, often the only way Mullins gets a hands-on look at how the book is resonating with readers. Kent also occasionally sends small gifts at Christmas and flowers when a book is finally finished.

BEST SELLER TIP

She Learned to Speak First

Carol Kent was a speaker before she became a writer. Her undergraduate degree is in speech education, and her master's degree is in communication arts. She has taught thousands of beginning and advanced speakers through her "Speak Up With Confidence" seminars, and she speaks often at events around the country.

Recently Kent was invited to be a keynote speaker by Women of Faith, an interdenominational women's conference organization that has reached 2.3 million women since it began in the mid-1990s. Speakers at the nearly thirty events per year include Patsy Clairmont, Luci Swindoll, and Thelma Wells.

"Developing a good speech is like writing a good chapter," Kent says. "I know I need a good introduction, or rapport step, in both."

In her speeches and her writing she knows to engage readers, to build warmth and agreement right at the beginning. She wants both listeners and readers to learn why they should stay with her to the end.

Creating a good outline also transferred from speaking to writing, as did the need for good filler information, such as quotations, statistics, word definitions, and compelling stories. Kent much prefers a story from her own life, but will settle for one from someone else or from a book or magazine if she finds an excellent source. A good conclusion is also a must for a speech, a chapter, and a book.

"I need to wrap up with an illustration that will touch the heart or challenge the listener to an action step. And I need an aim. What do I want my listeners and readers to do?"

Whether you're starting as a writer and moving into speaking or are a speaker moving into writing, "You take the one you are best at and build from there," Kent says.

"When both sides are quick with affirmation and choose not to be hurt when a suggestion is made, it makes the relationship stronger and the writing better," says Kent. "I think small gifts and words of affirmation when someone has contributed so much to your life only builds for the future."

Kent has these final words for writers:

"The more you are honest about your life, the more you reveal what is in your heart instead of glossing over it or covering up the imperfect parts, the more powerful the book will be. If you're authentic spiritually and personally it will strike a chord in the hearts of readers, who will tell others about your book."

Learn more about Carol Kent and her ministries by visiting www.SpeakUpSpeakerServices.com and www.CarolKent.org.

Chapter 33

Steve Laube
Agents in the Landscape of Publishing

Steve Laube

"I edit a concept, not a manuscript. I help the concept because publishers, marketing directors, and executives buy concepts. They rarely buy just content."

Steve Laube has seen the publishing business from many sides: He's been a bookseller, an editor with a Christian publishing house, and now an independent agent. He calls his role as agent a privilege, and sees himself as a facilitator and important cog in the machine of book publishing.

He can spend hours on the phone helping an author decide which of two publishers he should sign with, knowing that each house wants exclusive rights to that author yet neither house knows another is involved. He can help an author refine an idea for a proposal, pass along a rejection notice, or act as mediator between author and editor.

"It's a version of the United Nations," he says.

The role of an agent has matured in the Christian marketplace over the past ten years or so, says Laube. In the early 1990s there were two or three agents, at most, working in Christian publishing. That number has grown tremendously but still doesn't touch the number of Christian authors out there.

"When I was in the editorial position at Bethany House I worked with a lot of different agents and started to see the role grow and develop to where I felt agents were important partners in what I was trying to do as a publisher," says Laube. "When I made the decision to become an agent, I felt it was a natural step."

What Can an Author Expect from an Agent? Laube has several key things he offers his clients. The first is concept. He helps authors develop and refine content that can be sold to a publisher. That concept is reflected in a proposal that puts the idea of the book into a form the publisher hopefully can't resist. He scrutinizes, edits (some writers call it a massacre), and works every aspect of a proposal, as well any sample chapters.

"A client comes up with an idea, and he sends it to me. I help determine whether that idea is viable. A lot of times I'll bounce the proposal right back and tell him he needs to do several things," says Laube. "I'm helping the content, or concept, to be sold."

Authors should also expect solid career advice and action from an agent. Laube asks himself, "What and who is the best publishing partner for the next stage of this author's career?"

Laube offers his clients the available options, good and bad, renders his opinion if asked, then lets the client make the decision. Some have made decisions that turned out to be bad career moves. Laube is there to put things back together, a role he sees as part of his job.

"When I look at where to go next with an author, it goes right back to finding the right fit. Where's the best place for this content? Does it fit with Howard Publishing? Does it fit with Bethany House or Zondervan or Nelson?"

Once that decision is made and a manuscript is accepted by a publishing house, the next move in Laube's game is the contract. He helps negotiate everything from the amount of an advance to Internet rights to foreign rights, from royalties to the definition of "out of print" to ancillary products that come from the book.

"One of the roles of the agent is to think of the future implications of a situation, not just the current implications," says Laube. "You may have a relationship with a publisher now, but what if a foreign company swoops in and drops a million bucks on the head of the owner? Suddenly the only people who remember you aren't employees of the company. The only thing that remains is that piece of paper you signed, and if that is not well crafted you have to live with it. You signed it."

Laube sees his role as that of an author's partner. He's always a protector and advocate, but occasionally he's also pastor, mom, psychotherapist, drill sergeant, friend, financial counselor, tax consultant, and web master.

"Every agent is different, though. Each has his or her own personality. That's why it's important to find a good fit when looking for an agent— someone who believes in you, who you like and who likes you," says Laube. "But I'm an employee. I work for the author."

What Does an Agent   The employer/employee relationship
Look For in a Client?   works both ways. First, an agent is not a
                            rewriter or heavy content editor. Laube
recalls one relationship in which the author expected him to rewrite the manuscript. They parted ways quickly.

"I edit a concept, not a manuscript. I help the concept because
publishers, marketing directors, and executives buy concepts. They
rarely buy just content," says Laube. "It's a subtle difference. I am
working on making that proposal, that concept, land on an editor's
desk with a 'Wow! What a great idea. I just gotta have that.'"

Respect his time. A barrage of e-mails or phone calls each week or
even each day (Laube once got seventeen e-mails in a day from an
author!) is not respecting his time. One e-mail a week with a list of
questions, then patience when awaiting the reply, is not only good
manners but also good client behavior. Sure, contract negotiations
may merit a flurry of e-mails and long phone conversations, but
make sure that time is spent on business.

Be receptive to criticism. He offers comments and suggestions for
change to all his clients, and expects them to at least consider those
changes in the interest of creating the best proposal, or concept, as
possible. Negotiations are possible, to be sure, but respecting an
agent's expertise is also critical.

Expect rejection. Publishers reject proposals all the time, and an
agent's role is to pass along those rejections. It's not personal, and
it's not evil. It's just publishing. But an author who collapses at the
first rejection letter isn't going to last long in the business.

Be willing to work hard. Any agent also wants to work for authors
who are willing to work hard to produce their material. An agent's
reputation depends on presenting high-quality ideas, proposals,
and manuscripts to publishers, who in turn come to depend on
agents for viable manuscripts. Because so few publishers accept unsolicited manuscripts, an agent is a crucial go-between.

"What gets past my filter and lands on an editor's desk has been
well edited and I believe in it strongly," says Laube. "My reputation is on the line. If I constantly send them half-baked proposals,
they'll stop listening to me."

Laube's goal is to place at least 90 percent of the proposals he accepts; right now he's at about 75 percent. He also receives thirty to fifty new queries or proposals each week. One week he kept track of what crossed his desk. He received forty-one new queries or proposals: Seven of those new queries were from current clients; four were from published authors seeking new or first-time representation by Laube; thirty were unsolicited queries from never-before published writers; one of those thirty was worth a second look, but Laube didn't end up taking the person on.

If he were to have taken on the four established authors and the one beginner that week and kept up that pace, he'd have 250 new clients a year. Obviously this is impossible. Maybe he'll take on fifteen clients a year.

"It's a lot to take on even one new client a month," says Laube.

When do Writers Need an Agent?   Laube laughs at the usual question he gets from beginning writers: "Do I need an agent?" Of course, he says. An agent puts an industry professional at a writer's side as a safety net, an advocate, a helper.

The real question is "When do I need an agent?"

For Laube, it's when a manuscript is 95 percent ready.

"When the material is so good that when it lands on my desk I say, 'Wow! I can sell that,'" he says. "But if something lands on my desk and I find horrendous errors on the first page, technique problems, or the first three pages of a novel are internal monologue or backstory, I send a rejection letter. "

Writers spend untold time and energy looking for an agent when it should be spent on the book, Laube laments. Making a manuscript as good as it can be is the best way to attract an agent. That could mean hiring a professional editor or proofreader before ever sending a word to an agent, or it may mean paying for a manuscript critique at a writers' conference or through a critique service.

"With potential new clients, if I think their material is close but not quite there I'll send some ideas and and questions. Depending on how they respond to those questions, I may take them as a new client," says Laube.

Some writers, however, don't respond well. He's been screamed at, called names, told he wasn't a Christian, received nasty e-mails. Regardless of a manuscript's potential, Laube isn't about to put such an author into the hands of an editor.

"I'd like to be able to offer some help, but most people don't like to hear that," Laube says.

The key is understanding that an agent is just as important a member of a book's team as the writer and editor. Sure, there need to be more agents working with Christian authors and, yes, that number of slowly growing. There's also debate on whether the synergy of a large corporation is better or worse than the personal touch of a solo agent such as Laube.

Regardless, an agent has an important role in the process.

"There's nothing more fulfilling than taking an idea from conception to its birth and be part of that the whole time. I had that privilege at Bethany House, but by becoming an agent I'm no longer restricted to the needs of one house. I can now see the entire industry and place a manuscript with the appropriate house. It's a privilege to be part of that. I see myself as a facilitator and an important part of the process."

To learn more about The Steve Laube Agency, go to www.stevelaube.com.

Chapter 34

The Role of an Agent

Karen Solem

"Don't solicit representation until you have something you can send within a week or two. An agent doesn't want to see a draft until it is absolutely finished, in the most polished form it can be."

Karen Solem began by agenting ABA authors, then slowly started acquiring CBA authors as doors opened to agents in Christian publishing. In the years since she opened her own business, Spencerhill Associates, she's grown her CBA representation to about 20 percent of her client list. Her early career began in 1972 when she started working in the editorial department of a publishing company. She had worked her way up to Associate Publisher and editor-in-chief before she joined the secular agenting firm. She offers writers advice on the world of agents.

"Over the last several years, most CBA publishers began realizing that agents can be useful to their business, and these days most CBA (and ABA) publishers only take submissions from agented writers or authors they've met at conferences," says Solem. "CBA is a small percentage of what I do, but it is growing."

She looks for the same things from writers whether they're headed for CBA or ABA markets: a wonderful idea, a unique voice, and great expression of that idea. She's also looking for CBA authors who don't compete with anyone else on her list. With a limited number of publishers vying for manuscripts, it's hard to find new clients who don't compete with her existing list.

She also looks at personality. Can she work with that person? Will he or she be a good fit? A good author/agent relationship is as important as a good author/editor relationship. She recently turned down a potential client after receiving a demanding e-mail, deciding that if the person sends such e-mails when they aren't working together, the future doesn't look good.

"An agent mentor advised me to 'Think of it as a club. Clients should be people you like working with and who like you. If the relationship doesn't click, don't work together. Everybody will be a lot happier,'" Solem says.

Wrong Assumptions   She sees writers making several faulty assumptions when they look for an agent. The first is that the CBA market is wide open and, therefore, their manuscript will sell quickly for lots of money. The majority of CBA publishers publish under thirty novels a year and many of those lists are filled with repeat authors—it's not an unlimited marketplace. The advances paid are determined by how many copies the publisher believes it can sell. A great many books have print runs under 10,000 copies, which doesn't substantiate a large advance.

"Some writers pin unrealistic hopes and dreams on their manuscripts—becoming a published author does not automatically mean that your life will change. You will still have to pick up after your kids and you may still not be voted most popular. It's not a path to instant celebrity," says Solem.

Another assumption is about marketing. Some potential clients assume that a few well placed ads in *The New York Times, Christianity Today,* or *Focus on the Family* will guarantee success. They may also think that spending $1,500 on a publicist will get them on the CBA bestseller list.

"I can't predict the future; I don't know if that will work. But I do know if it was that easy, any publisher in their right mind would pay the money. There are no guarantees," says Solem. "With respect to nonfiction, the marketing section of your book proposal should not state the obvious like placing ads or a radio campaign. It should tell me what *you* are going to do, what's unique about what you offer.

- Do you regularly speak locally, regionally, or around the country?
- Do you have any special relationships that would guarantee you wider coverage, for example on the radio, and are those guarantees in place?
- Have you secured any big-name endorsements?
- Are you committing your own money to the marketing efforts and at what level?"

Publicity can be very difficult to get, especially for fiction. Publishers will want to see a self-starter.

- Do you have a nonfiction hook that will enable you to get interviews?
- Do you have any media contacts?
- Are you presentable?
- Do you have an attractive, effective, and up-to-date website?

Another assumption writers make about agents has to do with timing. Many writers present a book idea and an agent expresses interest and asks for the manuscript, which shows up months, even years, later.

"By then I may have three other ideas like it or two of my clients have gone in that direction or I have a full list at the moment but eighteen months ago I didn't," Solem says. "So don't solicit representation until you have something you can send within a week or two. An agent doesn't want to see a draft until it is absolutely finished, in the most polished form it can be. If you don't, you're going to lose your opportunity and you may actually lose good will with that agent for future projects."

Faith and Agenting For Solem, there is no separating her Christian faith from her role as agent. Her responsibilities to clients and publishers are the same whether she's a Christian or not. Anybody can call himself a Christian, she says, but that doesn't mean he acts it. She knows "Christian" agents she wouldn't turn her back on in a room, who poach clients and ideas, who will stop at nothing to get the client or deal they want.

"Just because you put the Christian label on yourself doesn't mean that's who you are or the life you live," says Solem. "What really matters is how you behave and what your actions are."

Growth and Change Agenting has gotten more difficult in many ways over the past five years, according to Solem. Because so many publishers are focused on nationally recognized authors, it's much harder for new authors to break into the business and get shelf space in Christian bookstores. Publishers are concerned about watching costs. That means fewer trips to CBA shows, limited PR and marketing budgets, less time and money spent making the author feel special.

Changes to come: Solem sees some smaller agents perhaps joining forces to create consortiums that can hire support staff, including PR staff and editors. More agencies will become full service, she forecasts, offering authors a full slate of services that could include manuscript editing and polishing and publicity. It's already happening on the ABA side. But the fundamental role of the agent won't change much.

"If you have one person totally enthusiastic about and committed to your work, that level of passion may be all you need to see something sell," she says. And CBA publishers are more and more comfortable dealing with agents.

Wears Many Hats   She sees her role as emotional support for a writer, financial advisor and occasionally moneylender, friend, bearer of bad news and good news.

"I think writing is a very difficult job. It's important that authors have feedback and that they have somebody to call," she says. "If an author is frustrated with her publisher, it's important that she have somebody to rant to. And it's important for me to be able to put those frustrations into perspective because they may not be realistic."

Solem has seen her clients through marriages and divorces, sick children and sick parents, and just about everything else. She tries to be there for them, listens to their struggles with life and writing, urges them to keep going. Some authors need constant hand-holding; some are content with two or three e-mails a year. Basically, Solem gives each author what he or she needs. What she needs in return is authors who understand that the process can be just as frustrating for her.

"I like my clients to communicate with me if they have a problem and let me speak with the publisher for them, particularly in areas outside of editorial," she says. "I see my role as a little like a facilitator."

She's found that publishing houses large and small, especially those in the CBA, communicate with the author first and with the agent only when contract negotiations or other business is necessary. But agents should be the first line of communication and defense so that they can run interference for the client if, for example, the author feels a new editor is necessary or an overzealous copyeditor has gotten involved. She often tones down negative comments from both sides, in the interest of keeping all parties happy and maintaining a constructive, creative environment for the client.

"I can usually find a nicer way to express a concern or positive solution to a problem that sometimes both sides can't see," she says.

Agents are important for a number of reasons. First, CBA publishers often won't read a manuscript if it didn't come from an agent. The agent should be a publisher's first line of defense in weeding out the less-saleable material.

Second, an agent can help an author better refine his or her idea to meet market needs. The agent knows what publishers are looking for and can lead clients in that direction.

Authors who have been writing for ten or fifteen years can use an agent to help reinvent themselves, to see beyond what they've been doing for years, and to look in new directions. Solem sees herself as a cheerleader, pointing her authors in the right direction and talking about what's working and what's not with their material.

Contract negotiations are also a key reason to search out an agent. While some agents can alienate a publishing house with huge demands and bad behavior, Solem's goal is to leave the author in good position with the publisher for the long term as well as negotiating a decent deal. Beating out that last $500 isn't as important as building a relationship.

Pet Peeve Solem has been ranting about one topic lately. She sees it in CBA and ABA authors, and and it is a common complaint from publishers: "Authors are writing four or six good books a year when they could write one great book a year."

Less can be more, she says, and publishers tend to agree. A publishing house could do a better job building an author if that author weren't writing several books a year for other publishers. Authors could concentrate on one or two books, building great plots and characters, instead of writing as fast as they can to be able to start on something new.

"I understand it's hard looking at a community of writers where this has been standard practice; a new writer sees it in established authors and sets up the same expectation. But it really is about the craft, about the process, about the book more than anything else. And most times a great book doesn't happen fast or easily."

Chapter 35

Lin Johnson

Wringing the Best Out
of a Writers' Conference
Lin Johnson

*"Today meeting editors is really key to getting published,
especially in the book field. Because many Christian publishing
houses are closed to proposals through the mail, you either need
an agent, which is hard to get, or you need an editor.
Your best bet is to go to a conference, meet an editor,
and be able to talk one-on-one about your project."*

Write-to-Publish is one of the most popular Christian writers' conferences in the United States. Writers come from across the country and the world to hobnob with their peers, meet editors, and learn the craft. Lin Johnson has been with the conference for over two decades, watching it go through several different formats and leaders until finally she took it over completely and settled it in its present form at Wheaton College.

Johnson now has two assistants who help periodically throughout the year on the conference, which lasts four full days. Cost for the conference and room and board is around $650. In 2005, 277 people attended.

For writers just getting started or a writer with a manuscript to sell, a conference such as Write-to-Publish is just the place to go. Beginning writers can learn several key things:

1. How to submit a manuscript in the right format. The right format means an editor will at least look at it.
2. How to find the right markets. Editors will be thrilled, not annoyed, at a manuscript that actually fits their magazine or publishing house.
3. How to write better. Who's ever done improving her craft?
4. How to come in contact with editors. Attending conferences offers a huge advantage to writers over merely reading books about writing.

"Today meeting editors is really key to getting published, especially in the book field. So many Christian publishing houses are closed to proposals through the mail, so you either need an agent, which is hard to get, or you need an editor," says Johnson. "Your best bet is to go to a conference, meet an editor, and talk one-on-one about your project."

Editor contact is also important to more advanced writers. Write-to-Publish is one of several conferences that offer an advanced track, which often means more contact with editors and more opportunity to network with other writers.

"As writers we're generally isolated," says Johnson. "We work in our home offices and don't have a lot of contact with other writers except at conferences, so that would be worth the price of the conference right there."

Johnson advises writers to attend one conference a year, which can provide a strong dose of inspiration to a writer at any stage of his career.

Preparing for the Conference   Preparation is key when going to a conference. Research the speakers and perhaps read their work, study the schedule to see which workshops to attend and which you might buy on tape or CD. Look closely at which editors will be there, then study what their houses publish and are looking for. Tailoring a proposal or manuscript for a specific house or magazine is always a good idea.

Preparing a portfolio is also smart. A simple folder containing your clips, resume, contact information, and manuscript or idea (written down) shows an editor that you are willing to do the research ahead of time.

Consider also tailoring your portfolio to different markets. For example, if you often write on family and parenting issues for a newspaper, use those clips in your pitch to a family or parenting magazine. If you also write straight news articles, include those when pitching ideas to a news magazine or website.

Johnson also recommends asking God for a teachable spirit. One of the most popular panel discussions at Write-to-Publish is with specialty markets editors. She gets countless comments from writers who were thrilled to learn of new markets for their work, such as greeting cards, curriculum, devotionals, or drama.

"So many writers come to conferences with a specific book idea.

If they can't sell it they think writing isn't what God wants them to do. But if you come with a teachable spirit, you may find all kinds of writing opportunities you hadn't thought of before," she advises.

Writers should also bring a manuscript in progress to take advantage of critique sessions, both scheduled and informal, as well as one-on-one feedback from faculty members. Johnson tries to match manuscripts submitted for evaluation with an appropriate editor, often resulting in sales.

While building relationships with editors is a key part of any conference, building relationships with other writers is also a plus. Perhaps that new friend will send writing jobs your way, pass your name along to editors, or even ask you to write something for them. Also, fellow writers know what you're going through, face the same struggles, and find joy in the written word.

Expect the Best from the Conference   Writers should expect several things from the conference itself:

1. Highly-qualified teachers. Johnson staffs Write-to-Publish with as many editors as possible, all with the ability to teach as well as interact with writers.

2. Good instruction. While small conferences can't bring in the big names, quality instruction can still come from lesser known writers.

3. Contact with editors, especially at larger conferences.

4. Feedback on manuscripts, especially at the larger events.

5. Hear God's voice through speakers, other writers, and editors.

"If you go with the expectation that God will give you some direction, He will," says Johnson, herself an active freelancer. Her freelance career began years ago at an early Write-to-Publish workshop. Her class assignment came back with suggestions for a few changes. She made the changes, and the editor who critiqued it bought the article. Since then she's written many more magazine articles, Bible study guides, and curriculum and completed numerous editing projects.

"I tell writers to develop a specialty—for me it's curriculum—that you're known for, but also be able to write other kinds of pieces so if a market dries up you can do something else," she says.

Getting on the Conference Circuit Interested in speaking at writers' conferences? While Johnson loads the Write-to-Publish conference with editors and agents actively seeking writers and manuscripts, she also has room for freelance teachers. She looks for writers with a lot of writing credits in the Christian market, and she requires a teaching tape unless she's heard you before or you come highly recommended by someone she respects.

She also expects prospective speakers to send a list of classes they want to teach. Johnson wants continuing classes, not just one or two electives.

"It's expensive to bring in a person from out of town. If I do that I'm going to use you," she says. "And I've found that writers will forgive an editor who is not a great teacher. They won't forgive a writer who isn't."

Why? "Because editors can buy their manuscripts and writers can't."

BEST SELLER TIP One Success Story

Wheaton College student Adam McCune and his father Keith, a missionary in Ukraine, had a manuscript to sell. Together they'd written a story based on the legend of the Pied Piper of Hamelin. Together they attended Write-to-Publish in 2003.

"Not too far into the conference, we were feeling very much like babes in the woods," recalls Adam. "Then we ran into Mark Tobey from Moody Publishers. He was interested in the idea of the book. He liked the historical setting and liked that the book was for a young adult audience. He made a number of suggestions."

Father and son took a week's retreat after the conference to reshape the entire plot. They wrote a proposal that included a sample chapter of the book, then sent it to four publishers with whom they'd made contact at the conference.

Moody Publishers responded positively. *The Rats of Hamelin* was released in Fall 2005.

"Write-to-Publish gave us a great refresher on writing basics such as plot and climax. It also gave us a chance to meet publishing representatives," says Adam.

"Before Write-to-Publish we sent proposals to publishers and agents and got nothing back. At Write-to-Publish we were able to get people to look at the book. It's how we made our book what it is," he says.

Jerry Jenkins
Terri Blackstock Lauren Winner
Karen Kingsbury
James Scott Bell Brandilyn Collins Angela Elwell Hunt Davis Bunn
Charlene Carson Sally Stuart Melody Carlson
Ann Baumbich
Jack Cavanaugh Nancy Rue
Barbara Nicolosi Justin Lookadoo
Dennis Hensley Dave Lambert & Lin Johnson

Conquer the Market: Building Your Presence with Readers and the Media

Chapter 36

Heart to Heart with Readers
Karen Kingsbury

*"First have a genuine heart for readers and,
second, find a place that is most genuine to act that out."*

Karen Kingsbury is a writer who embraces a unique blend of reader connection and marketing savvy. Her connection with readers is warm and personal: She talks with each person in long book-signing lines, she offers a Polaroid picture of herself and the fan, and she hugs and cries with a good many.

Her use of marketing techniques with the media and at venues such as the Christian Booksellers Association (CBA) convention is nearly legendary. A mug, a pen, or a notebook all serve to keep her name in the forefront. That translates into more media coverage and retailers handselling her books to buyers.

Her advice to writers is clear: "First have a genuine heart for readers and, second, find a place that is most genuine to act that out."

Kingsbury connects with her readers on a number of levels. First is on the dedication page of each of her novels. While her original intent was to offer her six children and husband a way to trace their lives through her books, the paragraph Kingsbury writes to each of them has put her readers right into her life.

"What the dedications do is give readers a glimpse of who I really am and what my life is like," she says.

She also includes a letter to readers at the end of each book. She tells readers why this book is important to her, what she hopes they took away from it, and her prayer for each reader regarding their relationship with Christ and attending a good church.

Kingsbury also connects through her website, where readers can send her prayer requests, read the daily devotions her family does, and participate in a reader forum. Kingsbury's personalized jour-

Karen Kingsbury Connects ...

With her books ... She connects readers to her family through the dedication page; she interacts personally with them via a letter at the end of each book.

With her website ... A reader forum, vehicle for prayer requests, and letters from Kingsbury are all connection points.

With her e-mail ... Kingsbury sends an email to her fan base listing when and where she will be speaking and/or signing books; she responds with personal notes to emails.

At book signings ... She talks to each person, takes a Polaroid picture, occasionally offers hugs and laughs.

At speaking events ... She offers books at lower prices, talks to people afterward, signs.

At CBA conventions ... Kingsbury spends time greeting retailers, giving gifts, and signing books.

naling is available to readers, as well as FAQs, tips for writers, and links to counseling sites.

She has two assistants who help answer the 300–400 e-mails she receives each week. Because many e-mails express thanks for her books and ask what else she's written, Kingsbury has produced a stock response that is sent in return. There are also many readers who request prayer for a specific problem in their lives. Either she asks her assistants to respond, especially if she's on deadline, or she responds herself. But each person is prayed for personally.

"Someone answers those letters personally. We do this as honestly as we can," Kingsbury says. "Generally I try to take a look at all of the letters that come in, but that's hard. My assistants red-flag the ones they think only I can answer."

Kingsbury also is proactive in reaching her fans via e-mail newsletters that list where she will be signing books or speaking. This is a relatively new outreach, but an effective one. She noticed changes immediately. A series of signings in New York City drew just three or four fans each, but she hadn't e-mailed her fan base about the events. When she e-mailed her fans about signings in Southern California, the lines were out the doors.

Kingsbury also uses speaking events and book signings to connect with her many fans. She speaks to each person, offering a smile, a hug, a compliment, a Polaroid picture. At speaking events she often brings books to sell at discounted prices.

"Book signing is a very spiritual thing for me. There is a very strong connection with God at the center. He has a reason for us to be together. Maybe it's to tell a woman she looks a little tired, maybe say 'That color looks good on you' or 'You sure have a happy smile.' My goal is that they leave more encouraged than when they came," she says.

The annual CBA convention is also a huge connection point with readers who also happen to be retailers. Their roles give them the unique opportunity to pass Kingsbury's books along to those who visit their stores. It's an opportunity she's not going to miss. She spends her own money on gifts she personally hands out as she greets myriad booksellers. She is just as generous with editors and publishers. Her goal, she says, is to make each person feel appreciated.

Marketing and connecting with readers are part of the same circle. "The first thing is having a heart for readers. The acting out of that heart becomes marketing. It's not successful when you say, 'I want to make a lot of money, so how can I market to these people?' Marketing isn't a successful starting place when you're talking about writing as a ministry."

Kingsbury's techniques may intimidate some writers, and she admits to feeling occasional cynicism from some who believe she's all about marketing. For those writers who feel uncomfortable with such hands-on relationship with readers, she suggests first praying for readers, and then using a website as a go-between.

"There are different levels of having a relationship with readers. Mine's way out there. I'll bet 90 percent of authors are introverts. I'm an extrovert so it works for me. There's a marketing level to it, but the deepest and first thing I know is that I fell in love with my readers," she concludes.

For more information about Karen Kingsbury visit www.karen kingsbury.com.

 **Putting Marketing Rules to Work**

Brandilyn Collins knows marketing. She spent twenty years in her own business creating brochures, logos, and other marketing materials for a variety of companies. She ran the business, which she started while in college, until her fiction career was well established. But after finding success as a writer of both women's fiction and suspense novels (see Chapter 21), Collins and her publisher, Zondervan, ran into problems.

"We kept coming up against this boulder in the path, and it was that I was writing in two very different genres," says Collins. "You build a readership in one genre and if you skip to the next genre you have to build a readership all over again."

She and her publisher decided she needed to focus on one genre, to develop a brand associated only with her. So Collins replaced an already contracted 3-book women's fiction series with a 3-book suspense series. She now writes Seatbelt Suspense exclusively, with the tagline "Don't forget to breathe … "

Her website was revamped to reflect this change, and her marketing materials—brochures, business cards, bookmarks, and postcards—are all centered on her new brand. She's even got a logo to help create one package that readers will recognize and remember.

"I always emphasize to an author that, as you get some success and sell some books, you need to realize you are your own company. Any company does some marketing, does some advertising, and that's the way it has to be. There is a certain amount of marketing and understanding of the business that you need to know," she says.

While marketing is in Collins' blood, she knows many authors don't understand the basics. She suggests teaming up with someone who does, even if it means paying her a few bucks to do some things for you.

Several of her key strategies include sending out a newsletter via e-mail to her fans, starting a blog about Christian suspense, and sending covers of her new books to church libraries, bookstores, and fans. She has Zondervan print 500 extra covers of her latest book; she then copies book and review excerpts onto the back and mails them out.

Her marketing background also helps her choose "very specific, hard-hitting words with personality to get a point across." Her writing is succinct, clear, and to the point.

Learn more about Brandilyn Collins and her "Seatbelt Suspense" by visiting her website at www.brandilyncollins.com.

Chapter 37

BUILDING YOUR PRESENCE ONLINE
Kevin McNeese

"Branding your name, not your book, allows you to switch the focus of your site without changing its address or spending money on a redesign."

Kevin McNeese believes authors can take a valuable lesson from the Christian music industry. Artists and their labels know what it means to create a presence online, to build community, to communicate with their fans.

"For a band or an individual artist, a lot more of their lives revolves around catering to their fans. The more the fans think they know that artist, the more likely they are to purchase future products by that artist," says McNeese, who got his start managing music promotions for FamilyChristian.com, the website for national retailer Family Christian Stores. "Music artists are the example for any author to look at in regard to promoting yourself online."

McNeese, who owns and operates KMWeb Designs of Meridian, Idaho, has created websites for a number of authors, including Fred Stoeker, Shannon Ethridge, Jen Abbas, Tracy Groot, Beverly Van Kampen, and Leigh-Anna Kaye.

Good Branding The first thing an author should do, according to McNeese, is create a strong presence online. Build a website that brands you as an author because your name should be what readers remember. Often authors want to create a website using their book instead of their name. McNeese disagrees.

"If book number two comes out and has nothing to do with your first book, your site is no longer applicable to your current subject," says McNeese. "Branding your name, not your book, allows you to switch the focus of your site without changing its address or spending money on a redesign."

Build   The second imperative is to build community. This
Community   means being active with your online readership
                   through interactive tools such as message boards,
chat rooms, interviews and regular e-mail newsletters.

An e-mail newsletter, which readers subscribe to on the website,
allows authors to keep readers updated on new books, speaking
engagements, and upcoming events.

"The better you let your fans get to know you, the more rabid
they're going to be when books three, four, and five come out,"
says McNeese.

An e-mail newsletter lets readers know you're active and still
writing. It's also a great way to harvest email addresses to be used
later in marketing new books and products.

Another way to build community is to offer a message board. At
JenAbbas.com, children of divorce can sign in and talk to each other about their experiences. Though McNeese says that new authors
may want to wait on message boards, more established authors can
really benefit.

Fred Stoeker, who had five books in print when his website went
live, has had huge success with his message board.

"It's a place where people can visit who are in the midst of sexual
confusion or need healing. His newsletter subscriptions have gone
up, the number of visitors to his website has increased, and it's really helped him out," says McNeese.

Consistent   Consistent updating is also important to creating a
Updating   vital website.
                   "I always recommend at least a monthly update
from my authors," explains McNeese. "Keeping that website updated is very important for getting that community up and rolling."

Each month Tracy Groot writes a new 4-5 paragraph introduction to her site, as well as a newsletter.

"It allows her to communicate with her reader base, to remind
them, 'Hey, I've got a book out right now so go buy it' and 'I'm still
here,'" says McNeese.

Monthly updates can also include book tour dates, new links to
recent articles you've published, updated resource lists, and thank-
yous.

"Keep that website updated and at least keep it looking fresh and
new," says McNeese. "You'll definitely be rewarded."

Website McNeese recommends several key ingredients for
Ingredients any author website:

1. Author biography. Personal information is great to include, but
keep private details off the site.

2. FAQ page. This can include questions and answers about how
you got started writing, where you want to take your ministry, goals
for this book, why you do what you do. Also answering general
questions such as "How do I get published?" is appropriate.

3. Information about your book, including cover photo, ISBN,
price, number of pages, and excerpts.

4. Ordering information, which can also include affiliate programs.
Many authors aren't equipped to process orders, so websites link
buyers to the publisher's site or sites such as Amazon.com, Fami-
lyChristian.com and others. Authors receive a small commission
from some sites when buyers purchase products after linking from
their site.

5. Resource links. Offer visitors links to resources pertinent to the
subject. Abbas, for example, links visitors to Focus on the Family,
articles on divorce, songs, and other books.
   "Think beyond just your book to how you can offer consumers
additional information," says McNeese.

6. Links to articles or interviews by you or about you that are available on other sites. McNeese recommends, however, that if possible put those articles directly on your site to prevent dead links
later if the article is deleted.

Dollar Cost is an important question when creating a website.
Value McNeese says this:
           "If you have a budget of $1,000, you can make a very
appealing, very robust site. A smaller site that contains a biography
along with five to six additional pages should run a minimum of
$500."
   Monthly update fees vary from person to person, job to job, so
be sure to research this when finding a designer. Additional costs

include the fee to register your domain name (www.yourname. com), site hosting, and costs for complete overhaul of your site if necessary.

But is having a website worth the price? What will the author get in return for money spent on a website?

"The biggest thing you're getting is the ability to promote yourself online to a world of people who are out of libraries and into home offices," says McNeese. "It's undeniable that the Internet has become our primary way of getting information.

"If someone has just read your book, they can set it down and forget about it, or they can go to your website and get involved with you. This is an active reader, an active fan who's going to be there when your next book comes out. People want information and they want it now. That's the world we live in. Consumers expect to find you on the web."

**Ten Simple & Inexpensive Ways
to Market Yourself Online**
—by Kevin McNeese of KMWeb Designs

1. Clean House before Inviting the Neighbors Over

Whether you have a site or need one, it's important to look at what you have before you begin to market yourself. Your website should look contemporary, stay up-to-date, and be easy to navigate. It should present your work in a way that is both entertaining and professional. Make sure your site can handle the flood of traffic that will come when you begin to focus on marketing. Is there a way to capture e-mail addresses? A way to sign up to receive e-mail newsletters? A way to count visitors, a place for visitors to e-mail you?

2. Your Best Brand Is Your Name

The best brand to build is your name, not your current theme, and your domain name should reflect this. This will give you the freedom to promote your latest titles and update the theme of the site with each release. It also makes it easier for people to find you through search engines, especially if you have written multiple titles.

3. Your Site Must Be Easy to Find

As soon as you have an established site, make sure your publisher and publicists know. Your domain name should be in all future editions of your books and accessible by a link from the publisher's site. Make sure the publisher and/or publicist also include it in magazine ads, press releases, postcards, and the like.

Another way to help people find your website is to add a signature line to your email with your full website address (http://www.yourname.com). One click and people have access to your site.

Your web developer should submit your site to search engines, along with configuring your pages with keywords and descriptions (called "meta tags") so that your site is search friendly. They should be providing this service as part of the initial design process, as sometimes it can take up to six months for a site to be registered on a search engine.

4. Build a Community and Make Yourself Available

A message board is a great way to connect you to your visitors and them to each other. Visitors register to participate in ongoing conversations that they either start themselves or jump into. When building your message board, first focus on the topics you write about and then provide areas in which members can broaden their discussions. Once your community is established, spend time each week interacting with your readers.

Ask visitors to fill out surveys about the topics you write about. You can also provide a Q&A section where readers submit questions to you via e-mail and you post your answers. Invite readers to submit reviews of your work and post them on the site.

5. Build an E-Mail Mailing List

The key advantage of e-mail marketing is that it enables you to contact your readers instead of forcing them to contact you. This is useful when something important happens such as the release of a new title, a review in a prominent venue, or author tour details. It's fast and cheap!

Collect addresses by allowing readers to subscribe directly from your site. Also hold contests. Give readers the ability to win a signed copy of one of your books, or partner with your publisher to give away something of value, such as an eBook viewer. When visitors enter the contest, capture their e-mail addresses and automatically subscribe them to your newsletter. (Be sure to inform them that, when they enter, they subscribe.)

Promote your e-mail newsletter wherever possible. You should have a short sentence in your e-mail signature such as "Get the latest updates direct from my site! Sign up for my newsletter here!" This gives everyone you come in contact with an opportunity to join without forcing the issue. Also, provide those who attend your speaking engagements with a way to sign up to receive your e-mail newsletter.

Once you have an established list, use it. Send out a quick monthly update. Press releases, reviews of your latest work, sneak peaks on future releases, sample chapters and site updates make great content for e-mail newsletters. Don't let readers forget about you, but make sure you use good e-mail etiquette. Never add addresses to your list unless they have specifically asked to be included (or informed they would be), and make it easy to unsubscribe.

6. The Importance of Networking with Links

A link is a connecting point from one site to another. Inviting readers to browse other sites where they can purchase your books, find useful information or meet other writers is a great way to add more relevant content to your site.

Figure out who your public is, then surf the net to find websites that reach your public. Offer a place on your site to link to resources and offer to trade links with these sites. Your web designer should be able to help you identify key sites.

Offer to trade links with other authors and present these authors on your site as ones you endorse to your readers. The more sites that link to your site, the better chance you have of showing up higher in search engine results.

Again, your publisher should use every opportunity to help promote your site via advertisements, postcards, press releases, etc.

7. Post Exclusive Content and Information about You

View your site as a way to get readers more engaged with what you do. Present more information than they can get elsewhere. This will establish your site as a destination point to get information about you.

Online journals are a great way to connect to an audience. A 3- to 4-paragraph update each month does wonders for keeping your site active and looking fresh. Also look at adding an extended biography and listing your favorite books, movies, and music. Ask your publisher for permission to post sample chapters from your works, and republish articles (with permission) that focus on your latest interest.

8. Partner with an Online Retailer

Find an online retailer that is willing to partner with you. While it may not be your job specifically, speak with your publicist about running a few promotions with retailers. Your two goals are to promote awareness of your products and your site.

Be willing to write original content or share what you already have. Offer contests that the retailer can run on their site or offer to provide signed copies of your book as giveaways.

Online retailers will be looking for traffic in return, so offer them a prominent link on your home page. In return, ask for a link to your site. You should be able to put together three or four 3-month promotions every year with various online retailers.

9. Make a Commission on Your Own Product

It's safe to say that everyone who visits your site has either read your book(s) or is thinking about doing so. Give everyone an opportunity to purchase your products. It's too expensive and time-intensive to set up your own store, but it makes sense to link to a well respected, established online retailer. Set up a "Buy" link prominently on your home page. How to link to multiple retailers or link to one exclusively for a short period of time via partnerships is explained in tip #8.

Make sure the online retailer has an "affiliate program": The online retailer's program supplies you with a traceable link, and you get a percentage of any sales made by guests who visit your site, click on the link, and make a purchase. You get a commission from whatever they buy, even if it's not your book! The percentage of sales varies from site to site, so find a program that best fits your needs and is comfortable for your target audience. If possible, work with a retailer that will help you expand your site.

10. Update, Update, Update

Maintaining your website is vital to your relevance online. It's a waste of resources to create a site, then ignore it until your next book comes out. A static site has value, but only to first-time visitors. Interacting with your readers monthly, weekly, or daily utilizes your site's full potential as well as your own.

Kevin McNeese lives in Meridian, Idaho, where he owns and operates KMWeb Designs. He has worked in professional web design and online marketing since 1999 and currently manages sites for various authors, artists, and small businesses across the nation. If you have questions about anything covered in this article, please contact Kevin at www.KMWebDesigns.com.

Authors' Sites Developed by KMWebDesigns.com:

ShannonEthridge.com

FredStoeker.com

JenAbbas.com

TracyGroot.com

BeverlyVanKampen.com

LeighAnnaKaye.com

DavidandDianeMunson.com

BEST SELLER TIP

Web Designer Kevin McNeese's Best Advice.

1. Have a website.

2. Maintain it.

3. Make sure it has a professional look and feel.

What to Look For in a Webmaster

1. Communication. Can you reach the person? Does he call or e-mail you back? Does she listen to what you want?

2. Price. McNeese recommends getting at least three price quotes.

3. Creativity. Do the designer's other sites show creativity? Consider carefully the designer's suggestions for your site.

4. Reliability. Do your changes get posted in a timely manner?

5. Reputation. Check references.

Chapter 38

Jana Riess

BOOKS ON REVIEW
Jana Riess

*"I don't want to give the impression that people
have to be radical in order to be reviewed,
but if they do something that's different or offer
a unique point of view, it certainly helps."*

J ana Riess has been Religion Book Review Editor for *Publishers Weekly* since 1999. That makes her nearly best friends with the FedEx, UPS, and Airport Express people who deliver the fifty to sixty-five books sent to her each week from publishers across North America.

Riess's home near Lexington, Kentucky, is an unlikely spot to be the center of the PW religion book review world, but that's part of the allure. Jana is home when her daughter gets home from school, and she is able to work around the family schedule.

"I think that when all these packages first started arriving, the neighbors were wondering what I was up to," she says. "I get pretty much any religion or spirituality book that is published."

The bulk of Riess's job is sifting through the books that arrive each week, determining which books to review and when the review will appear in the magazine, then matching each book with a reviewer, a "real art" she says. She also does occasional author interviews and feature stories on various aspects of religious publishing.

About 15 percent of the books she receives are reviewed in *Publishers Weekly*, according to Riess, although that percentage dips to around 10 percent during peak release times such as September and October. Reviews of religion titles run every other week in the magazine.

"It's depressing for the authors," says Riess, "but I think most publishers are very understanding about our limitations and how much competition exists."

Fiction titles might find less competition for review space, she says, in part because so many fiction titles are ineligible for review because they are part of a series. (Only the first book in a series can be reviewed.)

"Also, a lot of publishers have trouble sending fiction on time," she says. "Our deadline for receiving books is very, very strict."

Making the Cut   Riess looks at three basic things when considering a book for review:

1. Who the author is. She looks at the author's track record and reputation. An established sales record is a plus, though not a guarantee.

"We don't review curriculum or subsequent books in a series," says Riess. "A sales record is definitely in an author's favor, but that doesn't mean we don't review books by first-time authors. We do in almost every issue."

2. Who the publisher is and where the publisher is placing the book in its list. "If we get a note from a publishing house saying 'This is one of our two titles for the spring,' for example, that carries a lot of weight. If they're sending us ten books we obviously can't review all of them. So it helps when publishers let us know what titles they're putting their muscle behind."

Books also must be carried in mainstream bookstores and have a national distribution channel. This makes reviews of self-published books a rarity in PW.

3. The topic. Certain topics are over published, so it's hard to get a book in those categories reviewed unless it's saying something new or original.

"A book that is tackling something different and fresh is always really wonderful for us," Riess says.

But what makes a book fresh, unique, different?

"There's always a market for timeless spiritual issues—prayer for example. But if the book recycles the same kind of prayer advice I've seen dozens of times before, it's not happening," she says.

Books that know their target audience tend to be more focused and have a better chance of connecting with both audience and reviewer.

"Our reviewers are professional people who have read widely. Many have advanced degrees in religion, and some are pastors or rabbis or professors who have read voraciously. It's hard to impress them by doing the same old thing," says Riess.

Books addressing trends also can catch a reviewer's eye. But by the time a book is released a trend may be over, so Riess takes those books with a grain of salt.

She also looks for books that challenge typical thought in a subject area, that go a bit against the grain.

"I don't want to give the impression that people have to be radical in order to be reviewed, but if they do something that's different or offer a unique point of view, it certainly helps," she says.

Does PW ever get a response to a bad review?

"Let's reword the question," Reiss says with a laugh. "Has a month ever gone by that a publisher or author hasn't contacted us to complain about a review?"

Most complaints come from authors, she says. Publishers, who often do fifty to several hundred books a year, understand that every book is not a gem.

"I'm an author and I understand how courageous it is to write a book in the first place, but there are some authors who simply cannot let it go. They think any kind of criticism of their work, even balanced criticism, is an unfair and personal attack.

"It used to be that publishers could kind of bury a negative review. Only librarians or booksellers who got PW would see it. But now consumers have direct access to reviews through sites such as Amazon.com, so the stakes are a bit higher," she says.

A positive review in *Publishers Weekly*, or smaller venues such as trade magazines or newspapers, can do a number of things for a book.

First, it can bring much deserved attention to a book that might otherwise fade into obscurity. A review in PW can also increase sales to libraries and booksellers, though Riess is quick to say that a review is no guarantee.

"I've also had authors and publishers tell me that when a starred review has run, authors have been contacted by agents and publishing houses and, in the case of fiction, have been contacted by movie studios," Riess adds.

While a positive review can potentially be huge, the flip side is that a negative review can damage sales. Riess, however, subscribes to the school of thought that says any publicity is good publicity.

"We have found that consumers often don't remember if a review was good or bad; what they remember is the name of the book and that it was reviewed," she says.

Reviewer Responsibility   Book reviews are opinions: one person's opinion about one book. But with offering that opinion come some specific responsibilities.

Most importantly, reviewers must read the book thoroughly and well and come to it with an open mind. Reviewers must also be honest in their assessment of the book. Each review must be balanced and fair; no attacks against the author or polemics against the world in general. Criticisms must be specific and constructive, and reviewers must provide examples of problems if the review is negative.

"The reviewer is obligated to 'speak the truth in love,' whether they're reviewing for *Publishers Weekly* or for their local newspaper or church newsletter," says Riess. "Some reviewers find it difficult to say that a book has a lot of flaws and here's what they are, but that all is not lost."

An editor's responsibility, according to Riess, is to make sure a review doesn't become a weapon in the hands of a reviewer. Even-handed criticism is one thing; angry ranting at the author and his or her stance on the topic is completely another.

"There are other reviewing outlets that have that reputation, but it's not productive and it's not PW's job," she says.

Riess has a stable of about thirty-five religion reviewers around the country. Some specialize in particular religions or branches within those religions, so they don't review books that often. Others stay busy reviewing titles in the general Christian market. Most are referred by other reviewers, and almost all have an extensive list of things they've authored, whether books or magazine or newspaper articles. While Riess gets many requests to review for the magazine, most often the answer is no. It's not because of lack of expertise or experience, but because she just doesn't need more reviewers.

Riess and PW are especially careful to avoid conflicts of interest.

"Most of the reviewers are active writers and a lot of them are published authors, so I have to make sure not to send them books by publishers they've published with and, of course, never to send them books by authors they know personally. That's an absolute no no," says Riess.

The bottom line is that Riess trusts her reviewers to be honest about potential conflicts of interest, to read the entire book, to write their own copy, and to make PW's very strict deadlines. Reviewers trust her to edit well and judiciously, to choose books wisely.

"Our task is not to evaluate the world of a particular religion or its people. Our task is to evaluate the merits of a single book."

Riess is author of *What Would Buffy Do? A Vampire Slayer as Spiritual Guide* (Jossey-Bass, 2004) and *Mormonism for Dummies* (For Dummies, 2005).

BEST SELLER TIP

An Afterlife for Review Copies

What happens to all the books received by *Publishers Weekly*? Bound galleys are recycled, never sold online or given to bookstores. When Riess receives finished copies of books, one copy may go to the reviewer. She keeps a copy for about a year of all books that received a starred review. All other finished books are donated. Academic religious books go to a theological library in mainland China, and many others go to public libraries.

"These books serve a purpose. People who might not otherwise have access to them now do, and that's definitely something that PW should support," says Riess.

Chapter 39

GRASSROOTS MARKETING FROM THE HEART

Jen Abbas

"Having a sense of ownership about promotion is just as important to the success of a book as writing a great book. This means that even though an author's team may include editors, a marketing director, a publicist and possibly an agent, ultimately it is up to the author to make sure he or she is doing at least one thing every day to get the word out about her book."

Jen Abbas is author of *Generation Ex: Adult Children of Divorce and the Healing of Our Pain* (WaterBrook Press, a division of Random House, 2004). She is passionate about her topic, her book, and reaching fellow children of divorce. To reach her target audience, Abbas created a website, marketing materials, and tapped into the blogosphere. She is now working on a book describing 366 marketing ideas that any author can use, tentatively titled *Promoting Your Book Day by Day*.

Abbas, who is an associate marketing director at Zondervan, answers questions about writing and selling her book.

Question: *What is your philosophy of marketing for* Generation Ex*?*

Answer: My philosophy, and what I tell authors I work with at Zondervan, is that no one is going to be more passionate about a book than the author who wrote it. Having a sense of ownership about promotion is just as important to the success of a book as writing a great book. This means that even though an author's team may include editors, a marketing director, a publicist, and possibly an agent, ultimately it is up to the author to make sure he or she is doing at least one thing every day to get the word out about the book.

Question: *What steps did you take, even before it was published, to make potential markets aware of your book?*

Answer: I created a personal promotion plan while I was still in the writing stage. It provided a framework for me to create marketing and promotions as ideas came up. For example, if I interviewed someone or quoted a relevant book, I added that person to my influencer list. After the book was released, I sent letters and copies of my book to those on that list to help seed the market.

I think research is the best way to find potential markets. For my book on the long-term effects of divorce, I talked to counselors, pastors, authors, and lots of adult children of divorce. I found my target audience through my own website, other websites, message boards and blogs, and everyday conversations. Everyone knew someone who had been affected by divorce, so most everyone I talked to had a thought to share.

I had postcards created once the cover was final. I always carry them with me so that I can pass them on as a reminder to those who express an interest. The postcard shows the cover, release date, description, ISBN, and my website. My website has a newsletter signup, so I was also able to send out a reminder when the book released.

I also made friends with the frontliners at my favorite bookstores and libraries. One mistake a lot of authors make regarding book signings is thinking the most important thing is to sell a lot of books. That's a nice goal, but, ultimately, your primary goal should be to connect with the manager and frontliners (sales staff). At your event, you have an opportunity to create either a positive or negative impression that will last long after you leave. If you complain about the turnout, the display, or the lack of sales, you can imagine the taste you'll leave in the mouth of that store's staff. Instead, make a point to talk to each person working the event. Ask them what they are reading. Thank them for their work. Look for a point of connection. They are the ones who hand sell your book, tell customers about you, and make sure your book is in stock.

Question: *How important has your website been in your marketing?*

Answer: The Internet has changed the way consumers shop. The first place a person goes to learn about a product is a website. An author MUST have a web presence if for no other reason than that it allows you to have a constant marketing tool. The web doesn't sleep.

I would say that 99 percent of my interaction with readers, and even potential readers, is due to my web presence. While I was writing, I had a section of my website dedicated to interacting with other children of divorce. In addition to a pretty thorough survey, I also invited visitors to submit poetry, share specific memories, and list songs, movies and books that related to different topics. They could either e-mail me directly or post their responses on a message board. Not only did I get great resource material for the book, but I also was able to create a network of readers with a vested interest in buying the book.

In addition to the "Contribute" section and message board, my site has a bio page, a book page (with detailed information on the book, links to buy it, endorsements, press releases, reviews, a PDF excerpt, an electronic press kit and other bits of interest to media and potential readers), and a resource page (with links to related books, ten tips for divorced parents, and web links.)

Question: *How important have radio interviews and speaking engagements been in promoting* Generation Ex*?*

Answer: Given my topic, radio interviews seem to be a good way to get the word out. People may flip around the dial and tune in because they know someone (or are someone) who has been affected by divorce. Nonfiction seems to do better on radio, but I can't really quantify the difference it makes. I sometimes see a jump in sales on Amazon.com, but only if I look within a day or so of the interview airing.

In an interview format, listeners learn how to connect their need with the practical help found in my book. I get frustrated when I tune in to an interview where the author never gives any real meat, just a lot of teasing to buy their book. I usually end up more frustrated and less likely to buy the book. I'd rather give listeners something to ponder and create a desire to learn more. The other thing to remember about radio interviews is that, if an interview makes an impact with the interviewers, they'll be referring to it throughout the day and in the weeks ahead.

I've seen more of an immediate impact through my speaking engagements. It seems that the longer the session, the greater the sales. It's the same idea: The more I share for free, the more interest I generate for readers to get the book.

Question: *What part do personality and life situation play in promotion plans?*

Answer: If an author is married and has kids and has a full-time job, she can't be traveling every week for speaking engagements. So it's a matter of personalizing your goals and prioritizing accordingly. I don't think an author can really answer this question for himself until he knows what is most important to him. An author who has to support a family through his writing and speaking will set different priorities than the single woman who writes because she has a specific message she wants to promote.

Personality is also an important consideration. For example, I'm an introvert by nature and have often joked that speaking is a necessary evil for authors. It takes a lot of emotional energy for me to prepare and present. It does deliver a high rate of return, but I don't have the personality to do more than one event every month or so. Radio interviews, on the other hand, I can do in my PJs with my dog on my lap. It feels like a conversation and I don't get nervous. I like the reward of personal connection, and radio interviews offer that to me.

Question: *What are the best things an author can do to promote her book?*

Answer: Promoting a book is a lot like evangelism—in the best possible sense. It's sharing something deeply personal to you with others you believe will benefit from the message. Most Christians will tell you that they didn't come to faith the first time they heard the Gospel. It's a lot of little things that one day add up. It's the same way with promoting your book. Sometimes you see the result quickly—a speaking engagement that really hits home with someone. Sometimes you never do. But what you can do is make talking about your book part of your life in the same way you make your faith part of your life.

Question: *What are a few seemingly good marketing ideas that you've found don't really work?*

Answer: One of the biggest money pits is placing print advertisements in magazines. Because the cost is so outrageous, you have to sell a bazillion books to justify it. Maybe 99.9 percent of books never recoup the cost of print advertising. Of course, most authors don't place consumer ads themselves, so I say this to help authors understand why publishers aren't placing those ads.

As far as what an author can do, the only marketing ideas that definitely don't work are those that cause a potential buyer to affirm a decision not to buy your book. To go back to the evangelism analogy: If an author takes the approach, or gives the impression, that friendship—or even a friendly interaction—is based on the other's willingness to buy or promote the book, then that author has not sold her book and increased the odds of selling even fewer books. No one wants to feel manipulated. If the content of the book isn't compelling enough to interest a potential reader, manipulation isn't going to help. And, in fact, that person is more likely to spread the word against you and your book. The snooty author at a book store is a great case in point. Snooty doesn't sell.

Question: *How important is branding and why?*

Answer: The word branding brings to mind a lot of different ideas. I define branding as the process of creating a specific response to a specific stimulus. That response includes emotion, trustworthiness, loyalty, and a bevy of other measures. There are several authors who have done a wonderful job of branding to connect their writing with their readers. On the fiction side, Karen Kingsbury is a master. You know that the characters in her novels are imperfect and the plot will revolve around that character learning to live with the consequences of imperfect choices. Part of the drama of her novels is that you care about her characters, and, as God's grace is revealed to them, the reader connects to Christ as well. Kingsbury ends her novels with a letter to the readers, sharing the inspiration behind the story as well as family news. Her website and marketing invite readers to be part of the process. For example, the book *Fame* includes characters named in honor of readers who visited her site and entered a contest.

On the nonfiction side, branding is easier, if not as warm and fuzzy. For nonfiction authors, branding is more likely to align with an area of expertise. For example, Rick Warren will forever be aligned with the pillars of a purpose-driven life. Gary Smalley is an expert on love languages. Stormie Omartian is known for promoting the power of prayer. Steven Covey is known for the *7 Habits of Highly Successful People.* Often a nonfiction writer with this kind of success, for better or for worse, does best when he or she sticks to writing books that connect with their associated topic.

Branding is important because it creates trust (or distrust) in the mind of the consumer. It creates the potential for a book to sell well, or not sell at all. Dr. Dobson has a much easier time selling a new book than someone like, say, Jen Abbas, because as founder of *Focus on the Family* he has a brand name associated with family issues.

Publishing is a business, and the reality of it is that in order to make a profit, publishers have to publish books that sell. And we live in a consumer-based society where readers make decisions based on the names they know.

Question: *How does your view of marketing your book differ from traditional publishers' views of promoting the book for several months, then moving on to more recent releases?*

Answer: Unfortunately, if a book is released with a traditional publisher, more likely than not the promotion of the book is going to follow the publisher's schedule more than the author's. It's not right or wrong so much as it just is. The reality is that the marketing and PR team have limited time and resources and need to plan accordingly. And the media outlets that publishers are better equipped to work with have deadlines and processes focused on the three months prior to release to three months after publication. Beyond that window, it's very difficult for a book to get prominent media attention unless it is tied to a specific news event. Some publishers do a better job than others of keeping an eye on the backlist, but the reality is that once the publisher's initial push is over, the responsibility for keeping the momentum going—and looking for those media tie-ins—falls squarely on the shoulders of the author.

If an author goes into the publishing process with a sense of co-ownership for promotion, I think he or she has an advantage over authors who see promotion as the publisher's job. For one thing, they avoid the letdown of feeling like their publisher doesn't care about the book because the author has anticipated the dropoff and understands it as normal. And because they have been involved in promotion all along, the promotional efforts can continue seamlessly through the author's initiative.

Question: *How important is marketing to smaller venues, as opposed to traditional huge venues such as* Christianity Today *or* Publishers Weekly *or major radio audiences?*

Answer: The Internet has leveled the playing field for authors to get the word out about their book. It's the easiest way to connect with potential readers. At the same time, the marketplace is changing. Consumers are more likely to skip over expensive ads in magazines. In fact, most ads you see in newspapers or magazines are promoting books that have already been successful, or are written by authors who have already experienced significant sales. When is the last time you bought a book solely based on an ad in a magazine? For the midlist author, word of mouth is *the* number-one way to get the word out. An author increases the likelihood of success by finding those influencers most likely to spread the word.

And that's why marketing to the smaller audiences, most often by connecting through a website, blog, message board, chat room, or e-mail, is vital.

Question: *What can an author do to market a book that's been out for a year or more?*

Answer: The first thing I say to an author whose book has been out at least a year is, "Congratulations!" With 130,000 books releasing every year, a good number never see their first anniversary. If sales exceed 5,000, that's another milestone.

With ego and perspective properly in place, the best thing for a backlist author to do is to make consumer awareness (that is, promotion) a way of life. Certainly not in a pushy way, but in a conversational way. Look for opportunities to connect with potential influencers wherever you go, and be prepared to give a business card, postcard, or even a free book to those most likely to become an advocate of your book.

Question: *Describe your journey to the writing* Generation Ex.

Answer: The inspiration for *Generation Ex* was created before I was born, shortly after my mom and dad met. My mom's roommate gave her a journal for her twentieth birthday. In her very first entry, she wrote about this guy she was dating, my father. After they were engaged, the journal became a partnered project as both Mom and Dad outlined their hopes for their life together and recorded memories of significant events. As the years went on, my mom started

BEST SELLER TIP

Top Ten Tips from Jen Abbas

1. Create a blog and post daily or at least weekly.

2. Maintain a website and update it frequently.

3. Develop professional postcards and business cards and always have them with you to distribute.

4. Ask yourself daily what *one* thing can you do to promote your book, and do it!

5. Look for opportunities to establish yourself as an expert on your topic. Do this via your website, interviews, and speaking engagements.

6. Make friends with retailers and librarians.

7. Be generous with influencers. A good rule of thumb is that a free book to someone who can tell ten people about it is a no-brainer investment. (Be sure to autograph it so they won't give their free copy away.)

8. Develop creative promotions through your website and/or blog, such as contests with your book as the prize.

9. Make a list of topics related to your book, and pitch articles based on each one to magazines, newspapers and e-zines.

10. Cultivate a supportive prayer team.

to look outside her marriage for fulfillment, and my dad became the primary contributor to the journal. When my mom left my dad for the man who would later become my stepdad, the journal became Dad's safe place to sort out his troubled emotions. During this time, Dad became a Christian and his journal entries changed as he sought God's counsel on the issues of his life. Dad also jotted letters to my brother and me for us to read at some future date as we sorted out our own issues. My dad penned the last entry on the day the divorce was final. The journal was placed in the same worn, blue box as their wedding album and buried amidst other dusty reminders of a broken past.

Fast forward a decade or so. My dad is remarried and his new wife is making his house their home. She happens upon the wedding album and sets it aside to give me the next time I visit. I receive the blue box after college graduation. Still reeling from my mom and stepdad's divorce, this unexpected personal history is too painful to process, so I relegate the blue box to my own collection of neglected keepsakes.

Fast forward two years. My friends are starting to marry, and I'm terrified to date. It wasn't a problem in high school, but I haven't dated since. I'm happy for my friends. I'm content to be single for now, but there's a lingering question I'm afraid to address. Am I really content to be single, or am I really too afraid to marry? I decide to meet with my pastor for encouragement. At the same time, I'm packing my things to move in with friends. I decide to go through every box to avoid the hassle of hauling items I don't really need. I find a blue box.

My heart is tender and receptive to do the hard work of looking back. Looking at my parents' wedding pictures for the first time unleashes a flood of memories and emotions I didn't realize I was capable of feeling. I had been emotionally shut off for years. I was both encouraged and terrified. Then I saw the journal.

One characteristic I inherited from both my parents is less than precise handwriting. Now I see that trait as a God-gift. I had recently acquired a laptop and decided that this newly discovered personal history could best be referenced if I typed up the contents.

For the next three months, as I had time and my heart could handle it, I typed each journal entry. This history was new to me. My mom and dad were both great about not speaking negatively about each other. However, they didn't speak about each other at all. I had a huge hole in my personal history, and for the first time I was hearing my story told from a perspective untainted by the end result.

When I became a believer in college I clung to the concept of God as my Father. Typing those journal entries, God the Father was close, whispering truth, revealing both the good and not-so-good traits my parents passed down to me. He also instructed me, bringing to mind Scripture that would have helped my parents take a different path, and reminded me of passages from books I had read and sermons I had heard. In a very tangible example of renewing my mind, God opened my eyes to see how I had conformed to the patterns of my parents' world, and redirected me to see how I could transform those patterns to develop more healthy relationships. I began adding footnotes to the journal entries, capturing these thoughts as they were revealed to me.

When I completed the transcription, I was armed not only with a greater understanding of my history and myself, I also had a solid understanding of how my parents' divorce shaped my identity and patterns of relating. I recognized themes and specific hurts that needed to be healed.

I didn't have all the answers that day. But that journal and my footnotes became a workbook as I sorted out the questions. I would focus on a theme, for example a lack of attachment, and dive into research mode to learn everything I could about community, belonging, and bonding. What I learned was added to the footnotes and later rewritten in prose form.

Over the next several years, this ever-expanding document continued to direct my times of personal reflection and study. It was a personal endeavor, shared only with my closest friends in snippets and on rare occasions.

In 2000, I was conducting interviews with artists and authors for Family Christian Stores. One day I was interviewing John Trent about the Heritage Builders, an organization that equips first-generation Christians to pass down their faith to their children. As he spoke, he used phrases and referenced concepts I thought were unique to me and my private project. I was so taken aback I started to laugh. John, quite irritated, demanded that I share why I was being rude. As I shared my story, John's countenance softened and he said, "Jen, you need to write a book. This is your life mission. Here's my contact information. I'm going to help you."

I ignored him. For six months I ignored the template proposal he sent me. But God used many, many situations to get my attention. He met every challenge, every test I threw out. It finally came to a point where I believed it was a sin issue if I didn't pursue publication. So I contacted John and we started working on a proposal.

It wasn't that I didn't like the idea of being an author. It was just that I would much rather write some happy Christian Living book than expose my deepest insecurities and reveal to the world that I don't have all my stuff together. Writing a book as personal and vulnerable as *Generation Ex* is like announcing to the book world, "Hey! Wanna hurt me? Here is a definitive and descriptive list of every sensitive spot. Now let me just pick up the knife and direct it to my heart." For someone with insecurity issues, the publishing process is not the place to look for affirmation.

Looking back, I don't think that publication was the success. The "win" was my obedience to do the thing that terrified me most. God wanted the opportunity to redeem my family's worst moments, but he couldn't do it because I wouldn't allow him to. He needed me to submit to what I heard very clearly as his will. In that sense, I think God allowed me to have a very easy road to publication—all things considered. I would have taken any closed door as an excuse to let it go.

John Trent and I worked on the proposal for a few months, researching statistics and selling angles, drafting the chapter content and order, defining the distinctives of this particular book and why it was important to add it to the sea of books on the market. We also crafted a short list of publishers to which John would write a letter of introduction for me.

Of those eight publishers, *Generation Ex* went to the publication board with four. Ironically, at the same time I befriended another author, Fred Stoeker, who wowed me with his vulnerability in *Every Man's Battle.* As I was negotiating with one publisher, Fred asked why I hadn't considered his publisher, WaterBrook Press. After a few miscues that proved to me that God was directing this, not string pulling by anyone else, WaterBrook offered me a contact.

For more information on *Generation Ex* and Jen Abbas, visit www. jenabbas.com.

Chapter 40

Finishing the Job: Publicizing Your Book

Jessica Westra

"When the author is done writing the book, the work is only half done."

J essica Westra has a publicity trick or two up her sleeve. She worked in the field first as a college intern and then as an account executive at a major West Michigan public relations firm. Westra moved from there to Zondervan, where she lead the way in getting authors and their work into the public eye. These days she's a freelance publicist, working part-time from home using those same tricks she learned through the years.

"I love to be involved with Christian publishing because it helps authors tell the story they feel they've been blessed with," she says. "I'm doing my part in that big process by being able to get the word out about their books so that others can be spiritually uplifted, learn something new, or be nourished in some way."

Jessica's job, however, is not done solo. The other key player in publicity is the author.

"When the author is done writing the book, the work is only half done," says Westra, who has worked on publicity projects for authors such as Philip Yancey, Fern Nichols, and Rob Bell.

Publishers expect a number of things from an author regarding publicity. First, an author should be willing to do media interviews, either on radio, television, or in print. While some books aren't so natural a fit for interviews—devotionals or novels for instance—there are other ways to generate media interest, provided the author is willing.

Authors must also be willing to promote their book within their own organization or in other organizations they are well connected with. For example, Rick Warren promoted *The Purpose Driven Life* within his own church circles first.

BEST SELLER TIP Definitions of marketing and publicity as they relate to book publishing:

Marketing—
Paid advertising and creation of posters, fliers, and other materials, website design and internet campaigns, and strategic use of money toward "shelf-talkers" and bookstore displays, often generated by book publishers.

Public Relations—
Organizing events such as media interviews, speaking events, appearances, and book signings with the goal of promoting both the author and the book, coordinated by authors, book publishers, and freelance publicists.

"I would say that the bigger the number is for the sales forecast, the higher the expectation that the author be willing to put personal time and effort into promoting the book," says Westra.

Publishers assign certain dollar amounts for publicity for each book, some receiving bigger chunks while others receive little or none. While this may not seem fair, the realities of publishing and sales dictate such decisions. It's also why author activity is so crucial.

For first-time authors, the publisher expects him or her to actively promote the book on their own. Building a speaking platform, increasing visibility and availability, and connecting with organizations that could purchase the book in mass quantities are good first steps. Publishers are also happy to send review copies to media outlets contacted by the author.

"The author needs to be forthcoming with what other skills, talents, and contacts he or she may have to make this book really fly," says Jessica. "The author also needs to have realistic expectations about the time and money a publisher has to promote the book.

"You have to trust the publisher's staff. They know the market well and know what qualifies as a 'big' book. But they are also willing to take some risks."

There's also a willingness to take a second look at promotion dollars and effort should a book really take off, often the result of the author working hard at promotion.

Westra's biggest lament regarding publicity is when the author is booked for a radio, television, or print interview, yet never mentions the book title.

"It doesn't help the book at all if you don't give the actual title," she says.

Authors need also to know the specific audience for the book and speak directly to those people in the interview. They are the ones who are most likely to buy the book. Another irritant to public relations people is a big-name author who won't take time to promote the book. But when such an author is willing to do an interview, "people are impressed that he or she took the time."

What Should an Author Expect from a Publisher?

1. A high-quality product. This applies to cover art and copy, binding, editing and even paper choice. When Dr. Michael Wittmer's book *Heaven is a Place on Earth* came back from the printer with covers that curled back almost immediately, Zondervan ordered a new printing. Make sure, however, that the publisher destroys defective books instead of unloading them at bargain-basement prices.

2. A good effort to get the book to the right buyers. If your book is for young moms, sales staff should be getting the book to organizations that sell to that market; publicity people should be looking for radio interviews targeting that audience.

3. Open communication with the author. While agents can be helpful in this regard, an agent as go-between can also muddy the communication waters, according to Westra.

The Word on Specific Publicity Vehicles

Westra has seen marketing disasters and successes, been delighted and surprised, been annoyed and frustrated. Here's her take on some of the best ways to promote your book.

Radio interviews. Self-help, parenting, marriage, and Christian living books are good bets for drawing radio interest. Political books, especially during the political season, as well as books on hot topics such as euthanasia, the Middle East conflict, abortion, and even hormone replacement therapy are sure to draw interest as well. Publicists set up the interviews, though are always happy to get suggestions and contact names from the author.

"Radio publicity is huge, especially for Christian publishing, but you have to make sure you mention your book title," she says.

Christian television. There are few opportunities here, according to Westra, but the ones that are there are pretty good. Major programs such as *The 700 Club, Living the Life, Hour of Power* and *Family Life Today* tend to be geared toward charismatic authors who have incredible life testimonies.

Internet. Getting reviews on places such as Amazon.com or other online sites can get a buzz going about your book. Encourage people who have liked your book to add their comments. Contribute articles to online magazines or websites, always mentioning the book in your bio. Position yourself as an online expert on your topic.

Magazines. "It can be very hard to get in the top Christian magazines because the lead time is way out. To get your book in the magazine during the 3-month window it's prominently displayed in stores means approaching the magazine months ahead of time," says Westra. "But take any opportunity you get, even if the article comes out a year after your book comes out."

Local media. Local coverage of your book shows other media outlets that you are generating interest. Clips of newspaper or local magazine articles should be included in publicity material because they provide credibility, perhaps furthering similar print opportunities. And people who hear you on the radio, who know you or know of you via your speaking platform or ministry, are going to buy your book.

"It's very important to do PR in your own backyard because those are the people who are going to spend the most time with you as a local author," says Westra. "It's really very fertile ground. It's especially important if you are a first-time author with a smaller-market book."

Local media coverage can also generate book signings and other author events, especially if a store or station knows something will be in the local media. And vice versa, a book signing can generate media coverage.

Book signings. Authors dream of long lines of adoring fans, the flash of press photographers, a good sturdy Sharpie in their hands. Sure, those kind of signings do happen, but sometimes it's three or four of your closest friends or folks who wander by who stop at your table.

Don't be discouraged! Westra says that even crummy signings still generate local promotion. Your book was prominently displayed for two weeks in the front of the store, advertising got your name out and maybe even a mention in the local newspaper.

"You should expect no one to show up," says Westra, "but be pleased as punch that you got local coverage. Try not to be humiliated or feel lonely or that no one loves you. You are loved, you got a book contract, and your book was promoted locally. That's huge. It's worth it just for that display in the bookstore.

BEST SELLER TIP Publicity "Don'ts"

1. Don't be a nag to your publisher; be a partner. Look for ways you can complement their efforts.

2. Don't get distracted from following the marketing and PR plan. Do what you said you were going to do, and gently remind your publisher to stick to the plan as well.

3. Don't be unrealistic. Don't think you are going to land on all the hottest shows or the front page of *USA Today* or the cover of *Time*. Humility goes a long way in this business.

4. Don't forget to say thank you—to your publisher, your marketing and PR team, your agent, and, most of all, God. That's who gave you a burning heart for the message in your book in the first place, right?

"Folks may not go to the signing, but they may buy your book elsewhere or at another time, or online, or they may ask their church library to buy it."

Special events. Perhaps your publisher has connections with leaders of organizations who hold large-scale events where you could speak or where a special book reception could be held. Book industry events, media gatherings, pastors' meetings, and church rallies all may be potential areas to think about when putting together your strategic plan with the publisher.

For more information on Jessica Westra Media Relations, visit www. westramediarelations.com.

RESOURCES

Chapter 1
For more information on *Writers in the Spirit,*
visit www.faithwalkpub.com

Chapter 2
For more information on *The Too-Busy Book,*
visit www.randomhouse.com/waterbrook/catalog

Linda Andersen recommends:
The Artist's Way by Julia Cameron
(paperback; Tarcher, 2002, $15.95)

A Place For God: A Guide to Spiritual Retreats and Retreat Centers
by Timothy Jones (paperback; Image, 2000, $23)

*Invitation to Solitude and Silence: Experiencing God's
Transforming Presence*
by Ruth Haley Barton, foreword by Dallas Willard
(hardcover, InterVarsity Press, 2004, $16)

Sabbath: Finding Rest, Renewal, and Delight in our Daily Lives
(paperback; Bantam, 2000, $16) and *Sabbath: Restoring the Sacred
Rhythm of Rest* (hardcover; Bantam, 1999, $24.95) by Wayne Muller

Chapter 3
For more information on Davis Bunn,
visit www.davisbunn.com or www.thomasnelson.com

Chapter 4
For more information and writer's guidelines from
Discovery House Publishers, visit www.rbc.org/dhp/

Chapter 5
For more information on the Left Behind series,
visit www.leftbehind.com
For more information on Jerry Jenkins,
visit www.jerryjenkins.com

For more information on the Christian Writers Guild,
visit www.christianwritersguild.com

Chapter 6
For more information on *The Christian Writers' Market Guide*, visit
www.stuartmarket.com. *The Christian Writers' Market Guide* is available at bookstores nationwide, or by visiting the website.

Chapter 7
For a brief bio on Dr. Dennis Hensley,
visit http://home.mchsi.com/~jnwatkins/hensley.htm

For more information on Taylor University's Writing Program,
visit www.fw.taylor.edu

Hensley's books include:
How to Write What You Love and Make a Living at It
(paperback; Shaw, 2000) and *Write on Target: A Five-Phase Program
for Nonfiction Writers* (paperback; Writer, Inc., 1995, $12.95)

Chapter 8
Zondervan's website is www.zondervan.com
Lyn Cryderman has written *No Swimming on Sunday*
(paperback; Zondervan, 2001, $12.99)

Chapter 9
For more information on Tracy Groot,
visit www.tracygroot.com
For information on Moody Publishers,
visit www.moodypublishers.com

Chapter 10
Carmen Leal's websites are:
www.thetwentythirdpsalm.com
www.carmenleal.com
www.writerspeaker.com
www.allaboutquotes.com

Chapter 11
For more information on Discovery House Publishers,
visit www.rbc.org/dhp

Chapter 12
For more information on Jack Cavanaugh,
visit Zondervan's site at www.zondervan.com/Books/
and www.stevelaube.com/authors/jackcavanaugh.htm

Chapter 13
Find Charlene Baumbich on the web at
www.dontmissyourlife.com and www.dearestdorothy.com
Get her free TwinkleGrams at www.twinklegram.com

Chapter 14
Visit Angie Hunt on the web at www.angelaelwellhunt.com

Also visit www.tonystone.com for examples of photos,
and www.discoveryourpersonality.com for information on
Myers-Briggs Type Indicator ® testing.

Chapter 15
To learn more about Terri Blackstock,
visit www.terriblackstock.com

Chapter 16
For more information on James Scott Bell and his LOCK system,
visit www.jamesscottbell.com or purchase *Plot and Structure*
(Writer's Digest Books).

Chapter 17
For more information about Melody Carlson,
visit her website at www.melodycarlson.com

Chapter 18
Nancy Rue's website is www.nancyrue.com

Chapter 19
For more information on Damon J. Taylor's books,
visit www.kregel.com

Chapter 20
Crystal Bowman is a member of the American Christian Writers
(www.watkins.gospelcom.net/acw1.htm) and Society of Children's
Book Writers and Illustrators (www.scbwi.org).

Chapter 21
Visit Brandilyn Collins' website at www.brandilyncollins.com
Her blog site is www.forensicsandfaith.blogspot.com

Chapter 22
For more information on Julie Barnhill's speaking and writing,
visit www.juliebarnhill.com
To find out more about Mothers of Preschoolers
(MOPS International) or to find a group in your area,
visit www.MOPS.org

Chapter 23
For more information on Real Sex visit www.brazospress.com
To learn more about Lauren Winner, visit www.laurenwinner.net

Chapter 24
For more information on Justin Lookadoo's ministry,
visit www.RUdateable.com and www.lookadoo.com

Chapter 25
For more information on Lorilee Craker,
visit www.lorileecraker.com

Chapter 26
For more information on Zondervan Bibles,
visit www.zondervan.com

For a brief bio on Jean Syswerda,
visit www.tyndale.com/authors/bio.asp?code=633

Chapter 27
For more information on WestBow Press,
visit www.thomasnelson.com
For information on Laura Jensen Walker's other books
and upcoming releases, visit www.laurajensenwalker.com
For further discussion on Christian chick lit,
visit www.faithfulreader.com/features/

Chapter 28
For news and information visit www.christianitytoday.com

Chapter 29
For more information on Act One, Inc. programs or
funding opportunities, visit www.actoneprogram.com

Chapter 30
Visit Baker Publishing Group at www.bakerpublishinggroup.com

Chapter 31
A sampling of reference tools:
The Elements of Style
by William Strunk Jr. and E.B. White (Longman, $7.95)

A Christian Writer's Manual of Style
by Bob Hudson and Shelley Townsend (Zondervan, $19.99)

On Writing Well
by William Zinsser (Collins, 25th anniv. edition, $14)

The Chicago Manual of Style
by University of Chicago Press Staff
(University of Chicago Press, $55)

The Little Red Writing Book
by Brandon Royal (Writer's Digest Books, $16.99)

Chapter 32
Learn more about Carol Kent and her ministries
by visiting www.SpeakUpSpeakerServices.com
and www.CarolKent.org
Learn more about Women of Faith at www.womenoffaith.com.

Chapter 33
To learn more about The Steve Laube Agency and its guidelines,
visit www.stevelaube.com

Chapter 34
Contact information for Karen Solem is available at
www.christianwritersinfo.net/tips7.htm

Chapter 35
For information on the next Write-to-Publish Conference,
visit www.writetopublish.com
For news and information on Moody Publishers,
visit www.moodypublishers.com

Chapter 36
To learn about Karen Kingsbury's books and contests,
visit www.karenkingsbury.com

Chapter 37
To learn more about KMWeb Designs and Kevin McNeese,
visit www.kmwebdesigns.com
He has designed the following sites:
www.tracygroot.com
www.jenabbas.com
www.fredstoeker.com
and www.shannonethridge.com

Chapter 38
For information on Jana Riess's book *Mormonism for Dummies*,
visit www.wiley.com/WileyCDA
For information on *What Would Buffy Do? The Vampire Slayer as Spiritual Guide*, visit www.josseybass.com/WileyCDA
The website for *Publishers Weekly* is www.publishersweekly.com

Chapter 39
Visit www.jenabbas.com to learn more about *Generation Ex*
and Jen Abbas.

Chapter 40
Reach Jessica Westra Media Relations at JWMR@hotmail.com
or visit www.westramediarelations.com

Other resources to learn more about marketing your book:
Sally Stuart's *Christian Writers' Market Guide* (Shaw, $24,99) and
1001 Ways to Market Your Book for Authors & Publishers
(Open Horizons, $19.99)

INDEX

A

B

M

N

O

Olsen, Ted 145–149
O, for a Thousand Nights to Sleep 134

P

Plotting a novel 78, 82, 88, 92, 164
Point of view 164
Portfolio 186
Proposals 174
Public relations 69, 219, 220
Publicity 165, 219–223
    Definition of 220
    Author expectations 221
    Publicity vehicles 221–223
    Don'ts 223
Publishers Weekly 203–207, 214, 230

R

Radio interviews 212, 221
Reader expectations 67
Recommended reading 12, 69, 225, 229, 230
Reference tools 229
Research Tips 34, 54, 90
    Sources 50–52
Revision/Rewriting 77, 165
Riess, Jana 203–207, 230
Rottman, Carol 2, 5–8
Rue, Nancy 99–102, 227

S

Screenwriting 87, 151, 153, 155, 156
Self publishing 36, 55–60, 78
    Negatives 56, 57
    Reasons to 57
    Rule of thumb 56
    Tips 59
Sera, Clare 156
Slush pile 160
Small publishing house 35, 62, 63
Solem, Karen 179–183, 229
Speaking 171, 220
Specialty markets 186

About the Author

Ann Byle is a writer for *The Grand Rapids Press*, various magazines, and online publications; she also reviews books for a major review outlet. She formerly worked for Moody Press as a copywriter, as a copyeditor and book review editor for *The Grand Rapids Press*, and as an advertising copywriter for RBC Ministries. Byle is an adjunct professor at Cornerstone University. She is working on a second nonfiction book, a devotional for teen girls with Bethany Hamilton, and a novel. Ann and her husband, Ray, a science teacher, have four children ages five to fifteen, two dogs, one cat, a bird, and three fish.